Contents

Teachers' notes	2	Flying paper plates	19
Air is everywhere	5	How strong is the wind?	20
Where is air?	6	Make a wind-sock	21
Air in spaces	7	Sailing boats	22
Air in an 'empty' beaker	8	A windmill	23
Making bubbles	9	Rockets	24
Bubbles in the air	10	Balloon rocket	25
Air and water	11	Moving air inside	26
Air pressure	12	Heating air	27
Pushing and pulling	13	Snakes and spirals	28
Flying fish	14	Candle flame	29
Paper moving in the air	15	Sounds made by blowing	30
Dropping things	16	Smells in the air	31
Using air to move	17	How clean is air?	32
Indoor kite	18		

Teachers' notes

The aims of this book

The aims of this book are:
- To demonstrate that air is all around and that air fills spaces;
- To demonstrate that moving air is powerful and is a source of energy;
- To demonstrate that when objects move through the air, the air pushes against them, offering resistance;
- To demonstrate that air pushes on things;
- To show that air has weight and pressure;
- To show that we breathe air in and out;
- To demonstrate that air is needed for burning to take place;
- To raise awareness of things which move or fly in the air, living and non-living;
- To examine some of the properties of air, for example; air is lighter than water; warm air rises; we can feel air; we cannot see, smell or taste air; wind is moving air.

Developing science skills

The teachers' notes, together with the worksheets, present an active, experimental and developmental approach to science investigations. It is important that the child's environment and previous experiences form the starting point for new learning. The worksheets, which may focus on one aspect of an investigation, should be read and discussed to clarify the main ideas.

Children will need time to test and explore the ideas as they develop skills of observing, interpreting and asking questions. Their questions may lead to further exploration and development of their knowledge and understanding. Children will need opportunities to reinforce their learning by sharing with and explaining to others. The worksheets will provide one way for them to organise and communicate their ideas.

Scientific background

This information seeks to help you to understand the scientific concepts and ideas covered in this book. It goes beyond the level of understanding expected of most children, but will give you the confidence to ask and answer questions and to guide the children in their investigations. Other information is contained in the worksheet notes.

Air

Air is a natural material which encompasses the Earth's crust. We cannot see air but we can feel moving air, for example from a fan or the wind. We cannot smell air although we do smell polluted or 'fresh' air. The changing weather we experience is contained in the Earth's atmosphere. The air presses in all directions and is most dense nearest the ground. We measure the pressure of air with a barometer. The pressure of air decreases progressively as the distance from the Earth increases. Air fills empty spaces between objects.

Air is made up of several gases including oxygen and carbon dioxide. All animals and virtually all plants need oxygen to live. Living things produce carbon dioxide as a waste

◆ ESSENTIALS FOR SCIENCE: Air

product. Green plants provide oxygen in the process called photosynthesis.

Other gases in the air are water vapour, measured as the humidity, and pollutants, such as carbon monoxide and sulphur dioxide which come from sources such as motor vehicle exhausts and industrial waste.

Moving air has kinetic or movement energy which can make things happen. The force or push of moving air can cause movement in objects, for example a windmill.

Page 5: Air is everywhere

Key idea: Air is all around us.
Developing the investigation: Encourage the children to look closely at the picture for signs of air. If necessary, steer them towards commenting on leaves and litter being blown about, the kite flying, washing flapping on the line and so on.

Page 6: Where is air?

Key ideas: Air is all around us. Air is inside things which look empty. We can feel moving air.
Extension activities: Encourage the children to share their ideas about things which have air in them. Let them find other ways of making air move. Take them outside to look for evidence of air moving. Let them move about to feel the wind blowing on their faces or pushing against them as they run.

Page 7: Air in spaces

Key idea: Air fills spaces.
Developing the investigation: Ask the children if they can see the spaces between the objects. Discuss with them what is in the spaces between the objects.

Page 8: Air in an 'empty' beaker

Key idea: Air fills spaces.
Likely outcome: If the beaker is plunged vertically into the water the paper should stay dry.
Extension activity: Discuss what would happen if the beaker were turned on its side under water, then try it.

Page 9: Making bubbles

Key idea: Bubbles are made of air moving upwards through water.
Extension activity: Let the children make a 'bubble timer' from a container with a hole at each end. How long does it take for the container to sink? Does the size of the hole make any difference?

Page 10: Bubbles in the air

Key ideas: We breathe in air. The air can be blown out into a mixture that forms bubbles. The bubbles are full of air.

Developing the investigation: Talk about how we breathe air in and out. Discuss with the children what happens to the air when we blow bubbles.
Extension activity: What would happen if they blew bubbles on a windy day? Would we see the direction in which the wind is blowing?

Page 11: Air and water

Key idea: Water is heavier than air. The air is always uppermost in a container that is half-filled with water.
Developing the investigation: Colour the water with food colouring to help the children to see more clearly what happens.

Page 12: Air pressure

Key idea: Air has weight.
Likely outcome: The ruler is more difficult to knock off the table when covered with the open newspaper. It is the weight of air pressing down on the newspaper which makes the difference.

Page 13: Pushing and pulling

Key idea: Moving air can push and pull things.
Developing the investigation: Explain that wind is moving air. Let the children experience the feel of air pushing against the card and pulling the plastic bag.

Page 14: Flying fish

Key idea: Moving air can push things and make them move.
Likely outcome: The fish should move along when fanned, especially if the tail is bent slightly upwards. Discuss what is making the fish move.

Page 15: Paper moving in the air

Key idea: The shape of an object may affect the way it falls through the air.
Likely outcome: The uncrumpled piece of paper will probably float down. The crumpled paper will drop straight down. If dropped point first, it should be possible for the cone to be directed on to a target.
Extension activities: Find out which shape will hit a target most easily. Suggest the children find other ways to make paper travel through the air, for example paper darts.

Page 16: Dropping things

Key ideas: Air pushes against falling objects. Different objects fall through air in different ways.
Likely outcome: The objects will probably fall in three main ways; floating, spinning or dropping straight down.

Page 17: Using air to move

Key idea: To sort pictures into two sets of 'living things' and 'non-living things'.

Developing the investigation: Ask the children how they think each object flies through the air and which ones are alive.
Extension activity: Encourage them to make comparisons between the two groups.

Page 18: Indoor kite

Key idea: When a kite is pulled along quickly, it rises into the air and is held in the air. Air pushes against the moving kite with less pressure above so the kite moves into the air.
Extension activity: What modifications can the children make to improve the design of the kite (for example, by adding streamers or using a different type or length of straw for the crossbar)?

Page 19: Flying paper plates

Key ideas: Air pushes on an object from all directions. Air enables some objects, for example a paper plate, to travel through the air.
Developing the investigation: Let the children experiment with different-sized paper plates, using various methods of launching, for example throwing with a spin. Discuss which ways keep the plate in the air the longest and which make it travel furthest.

Page 20: How strong is the wind?

Key idea: Moving air can push objects and make them move.
Developing the investigation: Take the children outside on a windy day and discuss with them any signs of the wind blowing.
Extension activities: Ask the children to test some more objects. Let them find out how strong the wind is on another day using the same objects. Ask them if they can tell the direction of the wind from how the objects move. Does the wind come from the same direction every day?

Page 21: Make a wind-sock

Key idea: We can use an instrument such as a wind-sock to find out about the strength and direction of the wind.
Developing the investigation: Discuss with the children where they might find a wind-sock. Ask them how it works and what information it can give. Let them test their wind-socks.
Extension activities: Ask the children for ideas about how to record the information (for example, a picture record for a week). Discuss ways of making a more permanent wind-sock. Ideas might include threading wire round one end of a tube of fabric.

Page 22: Sailing boats

Key idea: Moving air can push sailing boats along.
Likely outcome: The boat with the larger sail will move more quickly.

Developing the investigation: Small boats can be made using materials such as plastic trays, matchboxes and dowelling or straws for the mast. Challenge the children to design a boat that is steady on the water. Ask them how the sails can be tested fairly. Discuss why some sails are more effective than others. Let them record and display their results.

Page 23: A windmill

Key idea: Air can push things and make them move.
Likely outcome: The windmill should spin.
Developing the investigation: Make sure that the components are held loosely together on the wire. A card disc stuck to the back of the centre of the sail may help. Let the children find out whether it spins fastest when they blow from the front, behind or the side. Suggest they make a second windmill with the corners curled round in the opposite direction. Is there a difference in the way the windmills move?

Page 24: Rockets

Key idea: Air under pressure can make things move.
Developing the investigation: Encourage the children to experiment to find the most effective way to press the squeezy bottle. A short sharp squeeze is usually the most effective. Let them try different-sized containers. Smaller squeezy bottles will tend to shoot the rockets furthest. Let them choose whether to use standard or non-standard measurements to record the distance travelled.

Page 25: Balloon rocket

Key idea: Releasing air under pressure can cause an object to move.
Developing the investigation: Ask the children to predict what will happen and to describe what they see. Encourage them to note how the balloon changes shape as the air is released.

Page 26: Moving air inside

Key idea: Moving air is used in some machines.
Developing the investigation: Discuss the machines used in the home which use moving air. What does the air do? Is the air heated? Is it blown out or sucked in?

Page 27: Heating air

Key idea: Air expands as it is heated.
Likely outcome: The measurement of the balloon's circumference will increase as the air inside is heated and expands.
Extension activity: Ask the children what they think will happen when the air is cooled. Suggest they put the balloon in the refrigerator or leave it outside on a cold day. What does this tell them about cooling air?

◆ ESSENTIALS FOR SCIENCE: Air

Page 28: Snakes and spirals
Key idea: Warm air moves things.
Developing the investigation: Encourage the children to test the spiral snake in different places around the room. Let them find the best place. If possible hang the snakes up where they will move. Discuss what is making them move.

Page 29: Candle flame
Key idea: Flames need air. Things need air to burn.
Likely outcome: The covered flame will go out.
Extension activity: Repeat the activity with a large jar and a small jar. Ask the children why the large jar keeps the flame burning for longer. Discuss ways in which fires can be extinguished.

Page 30: Sounds made by blowing
Key idea: Moving air can cause things to vibrate and produce sound. The vibrations produce the sounds we can hear.
Developing the investigation: Encourage the children to make sounds by blowing using a variety of objects.

Page 31: Smells in the air
Key idea: Air carries smells to our noses.
Developing the investigation: Show the children the collection of substances that smell. Cover up the plastic cups. Can the children smell the substances? Now take off a lid. Can the children smell more easily now? What carried the smell?
Extension activity: During a cooking session, let the children describe the change in smell, for example, when toasting bread.

Page 32: How clean is air?
Key idea: Air carries pollutants such as dust and particles of soil.
Likely outcome: The tissue paper should show evidence of dust or dirt.
Developing the investigation: Before the children embark on the activity, discuss whether they think air is clean. Why we need to clean windows and cars. Where does the dirt come from?
Extension activity: Let the children wipe tissues over different surfaces, such as leaves and windows.

National Curriculum: Science

In addition to the PoS for AT1, the following PoS are relevant to this book:

AT2 Pupils should:
- investigate what plants need in order to grow and reproduce.
- take responsibility for the care of living things, maintaining their welfare by knowing about their needs and understanding the care required.

AT3 Pupils should:
- collect and find similarities and differences between a variety of everyday materials. These should include natural and manufactured materials such as air.
- develop an awareness of which materials are naturally occurring and which are manufactured. They should explore the effects of heating some everyday substances (in order to understand how heating and cooling bring about melting and solidifying).

AT4 Pupils should:
- talk about when and why they feel hot or cold and link the sensations of hot and cold with thermometer measurements, for example in air.
- have early experiences of devices which move. These forces should be experienced in the way they push, pull, make things move, stop things and change the shape of objects. (They should explore floating and sinking and relate their experiences to water safety.)
- observe closely the local natural environment to detect seasonal changes including weather.

Scottish 5–14 Curriculum: Environmental studies

Attainment outcome	Strand
Science in the environment	Energy – different forms, sources, uses; Forces – different types of force involved in movement; Weather and climate; Materials; Planet Earth.
Designing and making	Planning; Making; Evaluating; Presenting
Investigating	Finding out; Planning; Recording; Interpreting; Reporting

▲ Name _____

Air is everywhere

▲ What can you see?

ESSENTIALS FOR SCIENCE: Air

▲ Name _____

Where is air?

You will need: a squeezy bottle; a container of water; a drinking straw.

▲ Where is air? Is air all around us? Is air inside things?

▲ Put your hand over the end of the plastic bottle and squeeze it. What can you feel coming out?

▲ Put the plastic bottle in water and squeeze it. What happens?

▲ Blow down a straw into a bowl of water. What do you see? Where has the air come from?

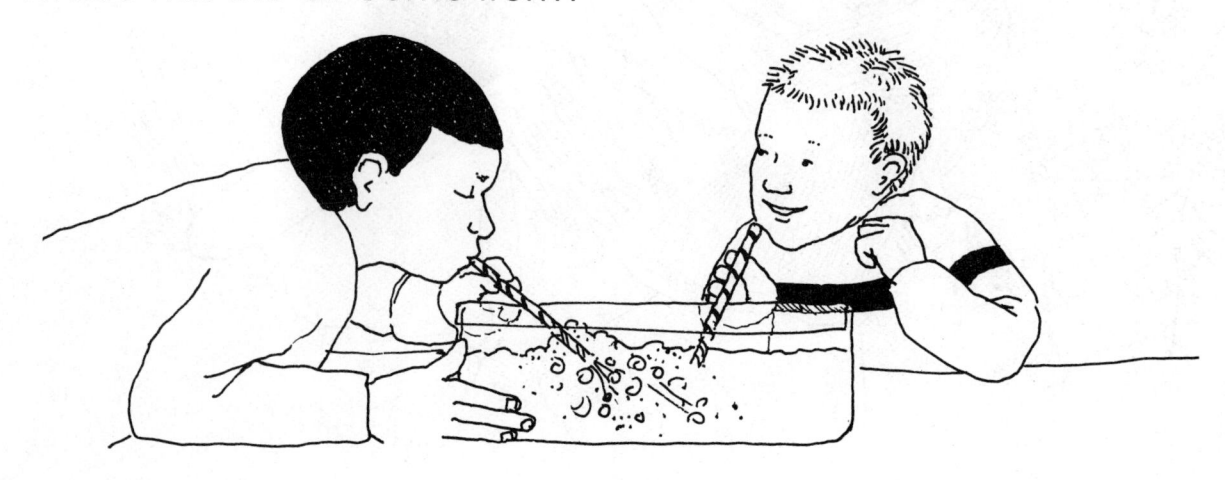

▲ ESSENTIALS FOR SCIENCE: Air

▲ Name _____

Air in spaces

You will need: some jars, each filled with something different, such as marbles, shells, sand or cotton reels.

▲ What is in the spaces between the objects in the jars?

▲ Which jar has the most spaces left between the objects? Is this the jar with the most air in it?

▲ Find out by pouring some water into each jar. How much water will you need for each one? How can you measure it?

▲ Put the jars in order, starting with the one with the most air in it.

▲ Where else can you see spaces filled with air? Draw some of them below.

▲ ESSENTIALS FOR SCIENCE: Air

▲ Name _____

Air in an 'empty' beaker

You will need: a beaker; a bowl of water; a piece of paper.

▲ Crumple the paper into a ball. Push the ball of paper into the bottom of the beaker.

▲ Turn the beaker upside down and push it under the water.

▲ Take the beaker out of the water and look at the paper.
  • Is the paper wet or dry?
  • What stayed in the beaker with the paper when it was under the water?

▲ ESSENTIALS FOR SCIENCE: Air

▲ Name _____

Making bubbles

You will need: a straw and a bowl of water; a sponge and a plastic bottle.

▲ Find ways to make bubbles in water. You could try some of the following:
- blow down a straw into a container of water;
- squeeze a sponge under water;
- put a container upside down in water and gradually let the air out.

▲ Now answer the following questions:
- what are bubbles made from?
- where do they come from?
- which way do the bubbles move?

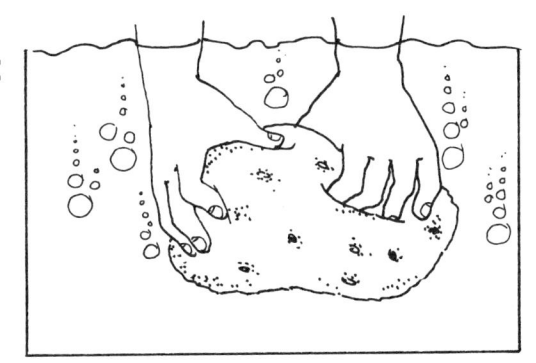

▲ In the space below draw a picture showing the bubbles. Add some arrows to show which way they are moving.

▲ ESSENTIALS FOR SCIENCE: Air

▲ Name _____

Bubbles in the air

You will need: bubbles mixture; some thin wire.

▲ Bend the wire in different ways to make some different shaped wands.

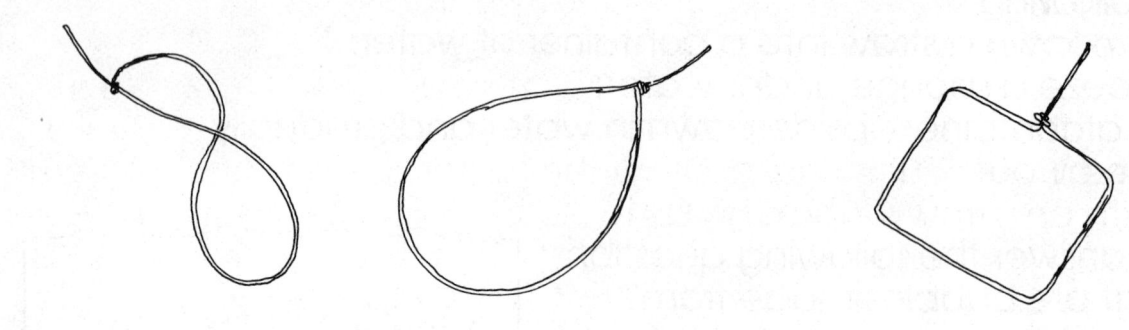

▲ With these wands, blow some bubbles. Watch what happens to them.

▲ What is inside the bubbles?

▲ Colour the bubbles below. Draw some of your own bubbles.

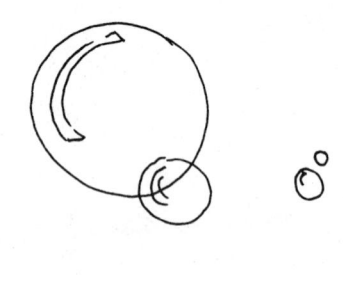

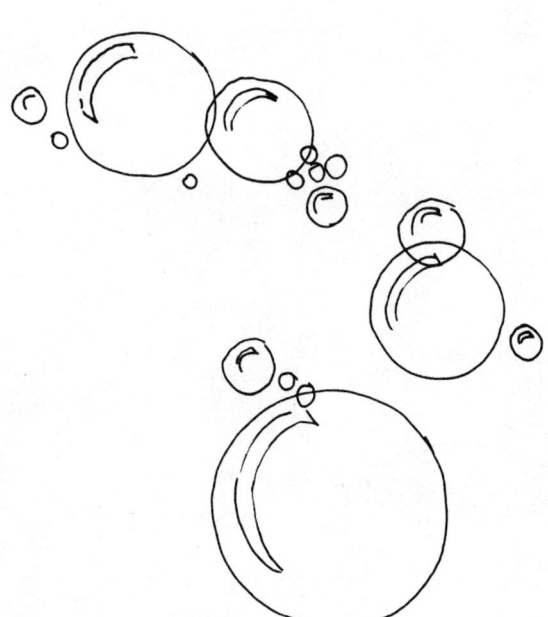

____ ____ ____ is inside bubbles.

▲ ESSENTIALS FOR SCIENCE: Air

▲ Name _____

Air and water

You will need: a jar with a lid; water.

▲ Half fill the jar with water. Screw the lid on tightly.

▲ Tip the jar different ways. Can you say where the air is when the jar is on its side or upside down?

▲ Look at the empty jars below. Imagine that they have had some water put in them. Draw the water in them and show with an arrow where the air is.

▲ What have you learned about air?

▲ ESSENTIALS FOR SCIENCE: Air

▲ Name _____

Air pressure

You will need: a newspaper, one sheet opened out, one sheet folded into four; a ruler.

▲ Put the ruler on the the table with some of it sticking over the edge. Put the folded newspaper on top of the ruler as shown.

▲ Hit the end of the ruler. What happens?

▲ Put the ruler back on the table in the same position as before. Lay a large sheet of newspaper over the part of the ruler that is on the table.

▲ Hit the end of the ruler again. What happens this time? Is it easier or more difficult to knock the ruler off the table?

▲ What made the difference? Was it because the paper is heavy?

▲ ESSENTIALS FOR SCIENCE: Air

▲ Name _____

Pushing and pulling

You will need: a large plastic carrier bag; a large sheet of cardboard.

Wind is moving air.
▲ Hold the cardboard in front of you and run into the wind.
▲ Now run into the wind without the card. What is the difference?
▲ Run into the wind holding the carrier bag behind you. What can you feel?
▲ Look at the pictures below. Colour in those that show the wind pushing or pulling against something.

▲ ESSENTIALS FOR SCIENCE: Air   13

▲ Name _____

Flying fish

▲ Cut along the dotted line.
▲ Fold along the solid lines to make a fan.
▲ Then colour the fish below and cut it out.
▲ Use the fan to make your fish move along.

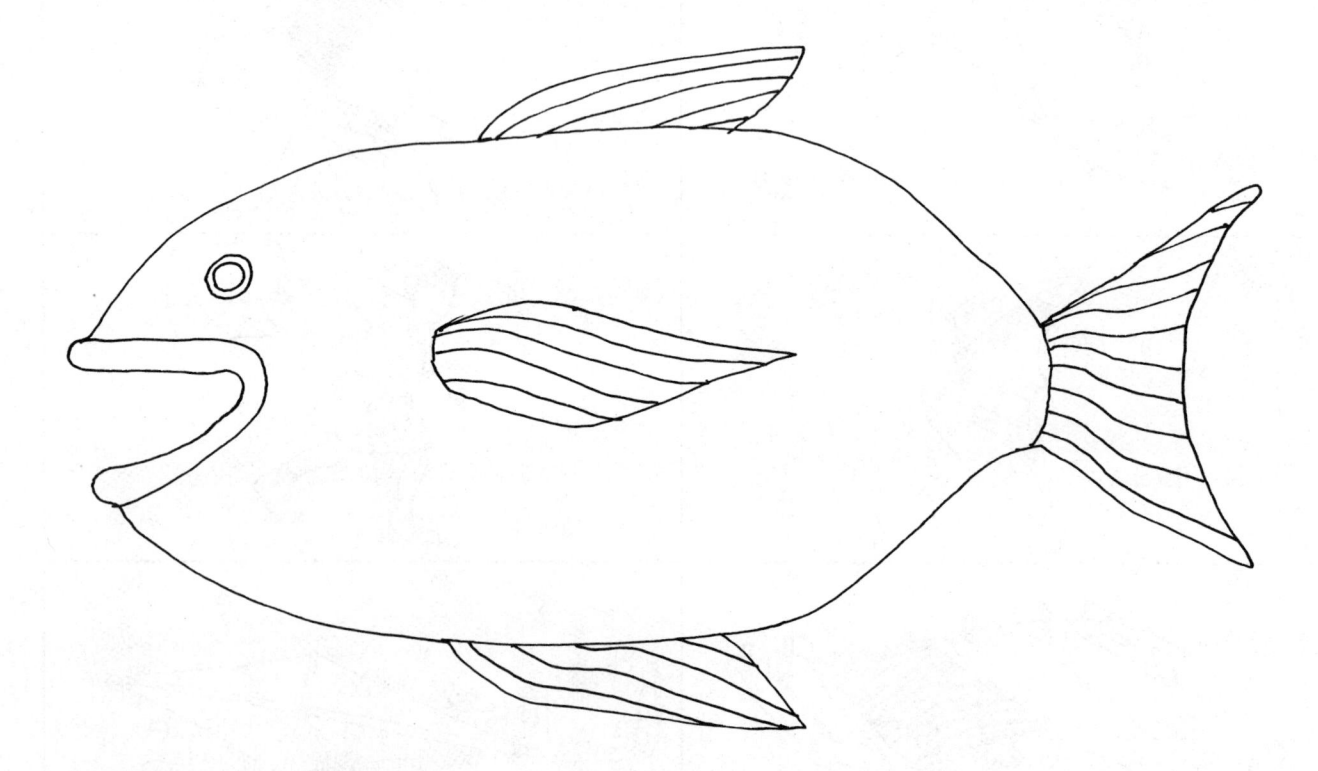

fold

▲ Make some more fish shapes. Make a bigger fan. Which are the best?

▲ ESSENTIALS FOR SCIENCE: Air

Name _____

Paper moving in the air

You will need: Sheets of paper; sticky tape; a stopwatch.

▲ Hold the sheet of paper as high as you can and let it fall.

▲ How did it fall?

▲ Now drop the same piece of paper and a crumpled piece of paper from the same height.

▲ Did they both fall in the same way?

▲ Now make a cone shape from a piece of paper and hold it in shape with sticky tape. Drop it from the same height.

▲ How did it fall?

▲ Does the shape make a difference?

▲ Do the same activities again and time how long each piece of paper takes to fall to the ground.

▲ Find other ways to make paper travel through the air.

▲ ESSENTIALS FOR SCIENCE: Air

▲ Name _____

Dropping things

You will need: a collection of objects, such as a paper bag, a polystyrene tile, a feather, cotton wool, a leaf, a piece of paper, a rubber and a paper clip.

▲ Drop the objects one at a time from above your head. What happens?

▲ Make sets to show the different ways that they fell.

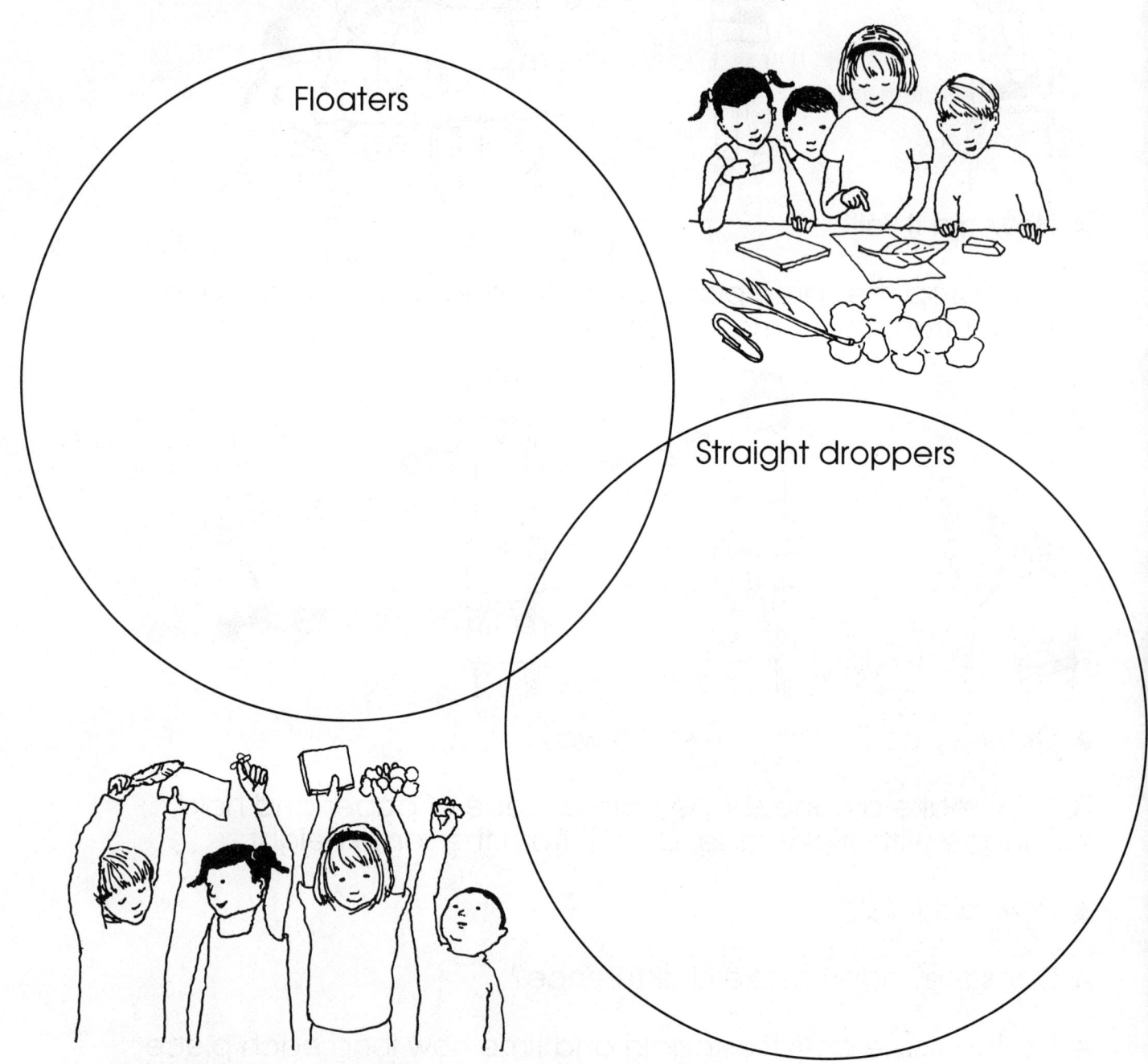

Floaters

Straight droppers

▲ Now look at your sets.
  • What kinds of things are floaters?
  • What kinds of things dropped straight down?

▲ ESSENTIALS FOR SCIENCE: Air   16

▲ Name _____

Using air to move

You will need: scissors; colouring pens or crayons; glue.

These objects can all move through the air.

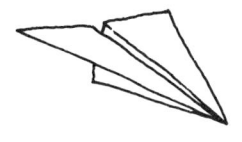

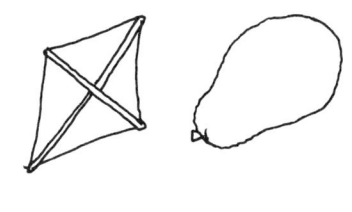

▲ Colour in the pictures and cut them out.
▲ Sort the objects into two sets, 'living things' and 'toys'.
▲ Stick the living things on to the picture of the garden and the toys on to the picture of the children.

▲ ESSENTIALS FOR SCIENCE: Air

▲ Name _____

Indoor kite

You will need: a piece of paper; a plastic drinking straw; masking tape; lightweight thread.

▲ Fold the paper as shown below.
▲ Tape on the straw and add the thread.

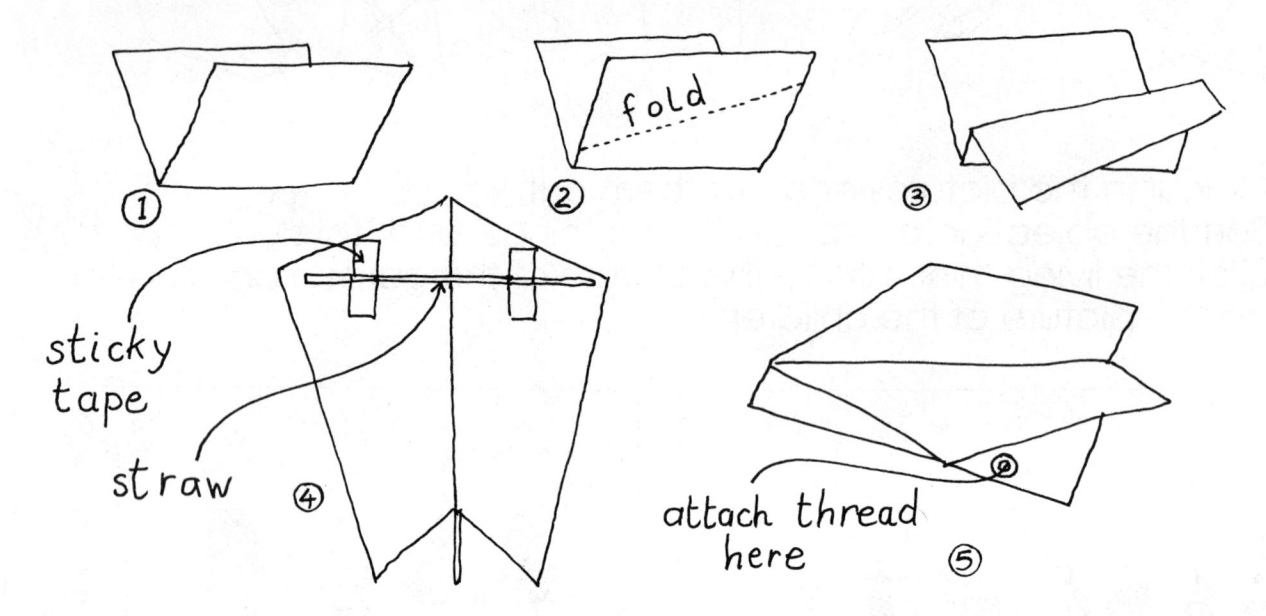

① ② fold ③

sticky tape
straw ④

attach thread here ⑤

▲ Move round the room holding the kite by the end of the thread.

▲ Answer the following questions:
 • What happens when you move slowly?
 • What happens when you go more quickly?
 • What is pushing against the kite and holding it up?

▲ Decorate your kite. You could add paper or plastic streamers.

▲ ESSENTIALS FOR SCIENCE: Air

▲ Name _____

Flying paper plates

You will need: paper or plastic plates of different sizes; a timer.

▲ Look at the plates.
- What shape are they?
- How heavy are they?
- Which ones do you think will fly away?

▲ Now test them outside.
- Which is the best way to launch them?
- How long do they stay in the air?
- Which stays in the air the longest?
- What makes them stay in the air?

▲ ESSENTIALS FOR SCIENCE: Air

▲ Name _____

How strong is the wind?

You will need: a collection of objects, such as a feather, a ball, a stone, a stick, a flat piece of paper, a ball of crumpled newspaper, an empty crisp packet, streamers stuck to a piece of wood or card.

Wind is moving air.
▲ Find out how strong the wind is. On a windy day, put some of the objects on the ground. See which ones the wind will move.

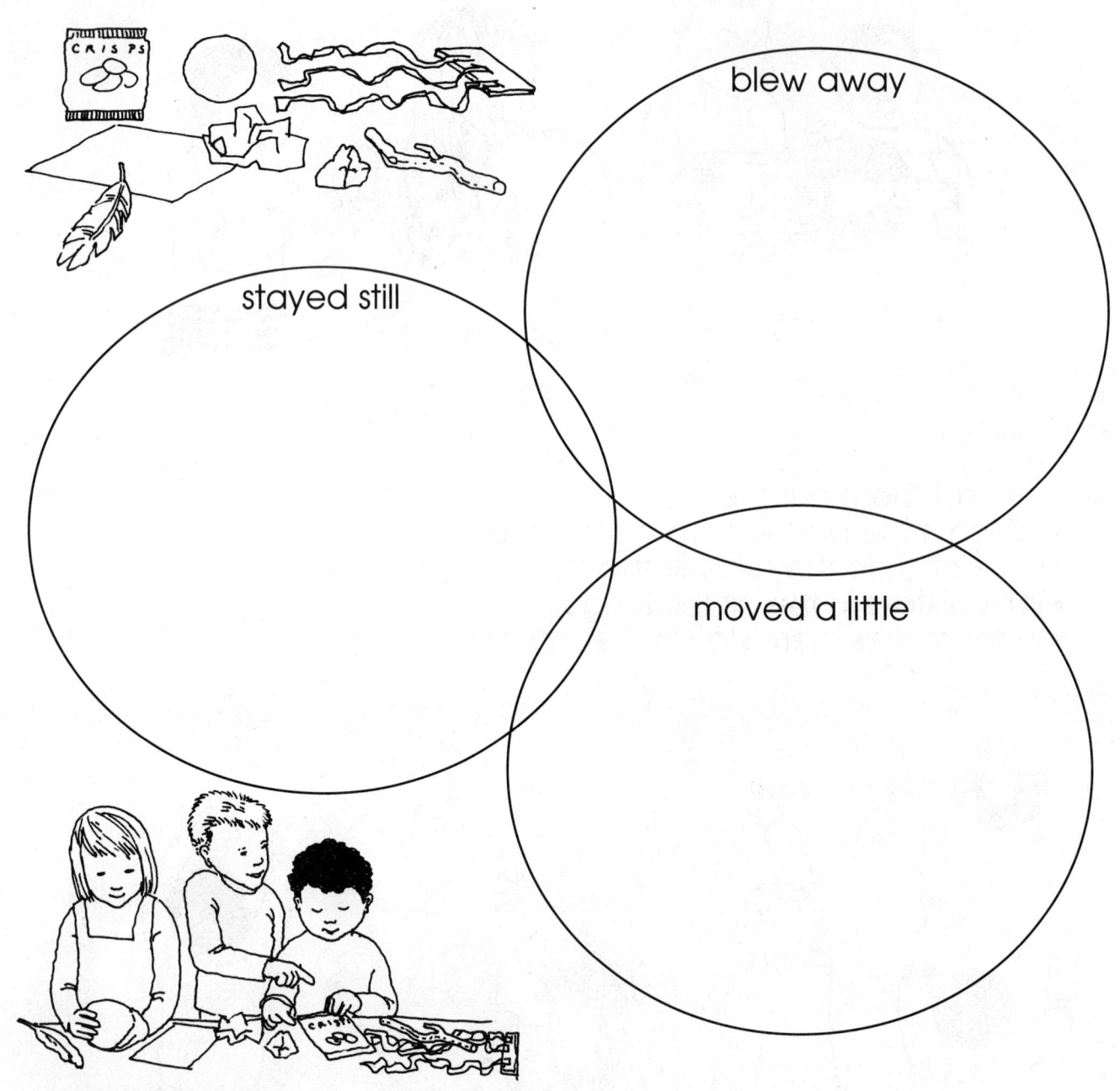

blew away

stayed still

moved a little

▲ Which objects move the most? Was it the light objects or the heavy ones?
▲ Test some more objects.

▲ ESSENTIALS FOR SCIENCE: Air

▲ Name _____

Make a wind-sock

You will need: paper; 50cm string or wool; sticky tape.

▲ Roll the paper into a tube like this.

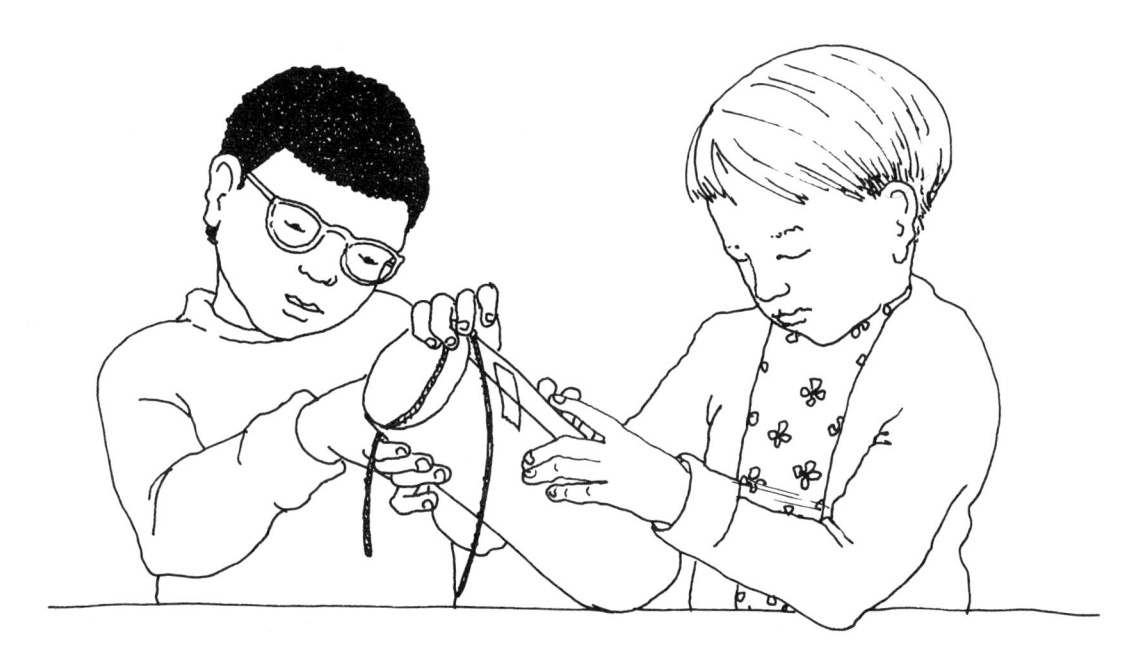

▲ Tape the top and bottom to fix them.
▲ Attach the ends of the wool or string to the top.

▲ Go outside and hold up your wind-sock. Which way does it point?
▲ Try it again on another day. Does it point the same way? Does it ever point the same way?

▲ ESSENTIALS FOR SCIENCE: Air

▲ Name _____

Sailing boats

You will need: materials to make the hull and mast of a sailing boat, such as a plastic food tray and a drinking straw; paper for the sails; a timer; a shallow water tray.

▲ Work with a partner to make two similar model boats.

▲ Add a sail to each. One of the sails must be larger than the other.

▲ Now put the boats on the water and blow them along. Which goes fastest?

▲ Draw the fastest boat here. Why was it the fastest?

▲ Design a better sail to make your boat move more quickly.

▲ Time the speed of your boat.

▲ ESSENTIALS FOR SCIENCE: Air

▲ Name _____

A windmill

You will need: paper; a drinking straw; a split pin; a plastic bottle; a fan.

▲ Make a windmill like this.

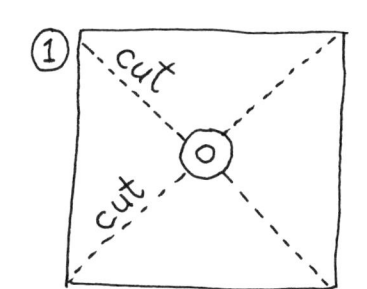

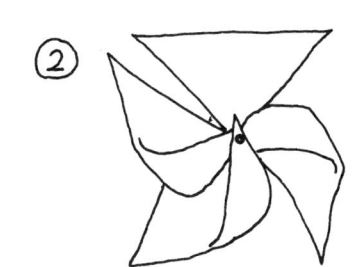

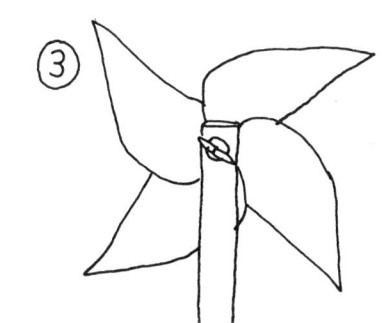

▲ Try different ways of making the sails turn.
  • Blow through the straw.
  • Pump the air from the plastic bottle.
  • Use a fan.

▲ What other ways can you think of to make the sails turn?
▲ Which way was the most successful?
▲ Which method made the sails turn fastest?

▲ ESSENTIALS FOR SCIENCE: Air

▲ Name _____

Rockets   ⚠

You will need: plastic washing-up bottles; jumbo-sized and medium-sized drinking straws; Plasticine.

▲ Put the jumbo-sized straw into the neck of the plastic bottle. Seal it with Plasticine.

▲ Seal the end of the medium-sized straw with Plasticine and insert it into the jumbo straw.

▲ Squeeze the bottle hard. What happens?

▲ Squeeze the bottle gently. What happens?

▲ Try some other materials to make your rocket.

▲ Answer the following questions:
  • How far did your rocket go?
  • Which is the best size of squeezy bottle for this?
  • What makes the rocket move?

▲ ESSENTIALS FOR SCIENCE: Air

▲ Name _____

Balloon rocket

You will need: a long balloon; an inflator; crêpe-paper streamers; a bulldog clip; masking tape.

▲ Inflate the balloon. Hold it by the neck. What will happen when you let the balloon go?
▲ Hold the balloon up and release it. How far did it travel? What made the balloon start moving? What made it stop?
▲ Pump just one puff of air into the balloon and let it go. How far does it travel?
▲ Now pump two puffs of air into it. Does it travel further?
▲ How far will it travel if it is full of air?
▲ Complete the graph below to show your findings.

▲ ESSENTIALS FOR SCIENCE: Air

▲ Name _____

Moving air inside

▲ Look at the machines at home and at school.

▲ Look at the machines on this page. Which of them use air?

▲ Colour in those that use air.

▲ Why do we need the machines that move air?

▲ Draw a machine that uses air and add arrows to show which way the air is moving.

▲ ESSENTIALS FOR SCIENCE: Air

▲ Name _____

Heating air

You will need: a round balloon; an inflator; measuring tape; a pencil; string or wool; a warm radiator.

▲ Pump air into the balloon until it is about half the full size. Secure the end.
▲ Measure round the balloon. Write down the measurement.

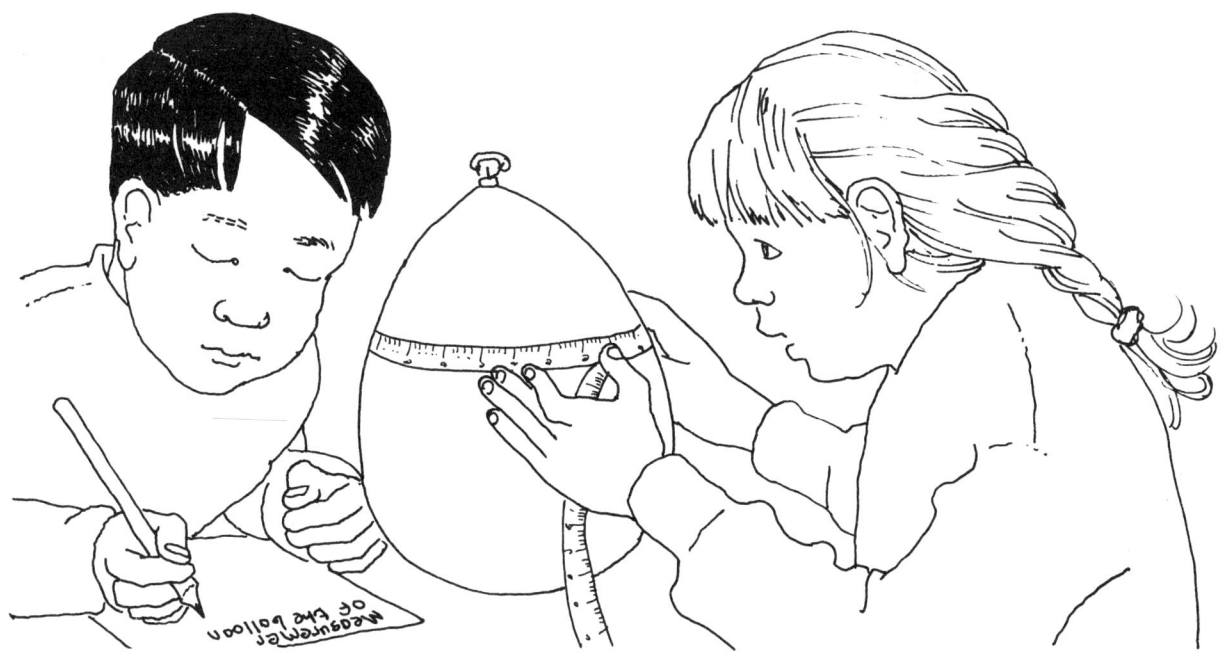

▲ Hang the balloon above a warm radiator for five minutes. Now measure the balloon again.

▲ How has the measurement changed? What made it change? What does this tell us about warm air?

▲ ESSENTIALS FOR SCIENCE: Air   27

▲ Name _____

Snakes and spirals

You will need: scissors; felt-tipped pens; thread; a warm radiator.

▲ Colour and cut out the snake shape below.

▲ Fix the thread to the snake's head and dangle it over a warm radiator. What happens to the snake?

▲ What does this tell us about warm air?

▲ ESSENTIALS FOR SCIENCE: Air

▲ Name _____

Candle flame

You will need: a large jar; two candles or nightlights; two baking trays filled with sand.

▲ Place a candle on the sand in the middle of each tray. Ask a grown-up to light the candles.

▲ Place an upturned jar over one of the candles. What happens?

▲ What do you think will happen if you do it again but cover the other candle?

▲ Try it. Were you right?

▲ Why does the flame of the covered candle go out?

▲ ESSENTIALS FOR SCIENCE: Air

▲ Name _____

Sounds made by blowing

You will need: a collection of wind instruments (pipes, recorders, whistles); empty bottles; paper; comb and paper; drinking straw.

By blowing air you can make different sounds.

▲ Try some of the musical instruments.

▲ Try blowing across the top of an empty bottle or blowing on a comb covered with tissue paper.

▲ Now try blowing on a straw flattened and cut like this.

▲ Design an instrument that makes a sound by blowing air.

My design

▲ How many different sounds can you make by blowing air?

▲ ESSENTIALS FOR SCIENCE: Air

▲ Name _____

Smells in the air

You will need: a collection of things with different kinds of smells, each placed in a plastic cup. Try an onion, coffee, lemon juice, curry, vinegar, a banana, an orange, disinfectant, soap, perfume.

▲ Do you smell something when you breathe in or breathe out?

▲ Do you smell something when you breathe through your nose or through your mouth?

▲ Discuss your favourite smells with your friends.

▲ Discuss the smells you hate.

▲ Record your findings below.

Nice smells	Nasty smells

▲ What carries smells to your nose?

▲ ESSENTIALS FOR SCIENCE: Air

▲ Name _____

How clean is air?

You will need: 3 plastic beakers; some white tissues; elastic bands; 3 pebbles or weights.

▲ Place a pebble in a beaker to weight it down. Stretch a tissue over the top. Hold it in place with an elastic band.

▲ Do the same with the other two beakers.

▲ Decide where to put the beakers to test for clean air. You could choose outside by a wall, inside the classroom or by a draughty window. Leave them there for at least two days.

▲ Look carefully at the beakers. How have they changed?

▲ Record your findings below.

beaker 1	beaker 2	beaker 3

▲ What does this tell you about air?

▲ ESSENTIALS FOR SCIENCE: Air

Contents

Teachers' notes	1
Notes on individual activities	2
What is water like?	5
What do we use water for?	6
What shape is water?	7
Running water	8
Water level	9
Make a siphon	10
Water surface	11
A drop of water	12
Drops of water on surfaces	13
Washing hands	14
Puddle puzzle	15
Water disappears into the air	16
The best weather for drying	17
From steam to water	18
Where does water come from?	19
Make a rain gauge	20
Keeping ice cubes cold	21
An ice cube melting	22
Dissolving things in water	23
Dilute a drink	24
Floating and sinking	25
Pushing water	26
Jets of water	27
Do seeds need water to grow?	28
Do plants take up water?	29
What did I drink today?	30
Make a water filter	31
Water in our homes	32

Teachers' notes

Aims of this book

The aims of this book are:
- To raise awareness of the various uses of water.
- To examine some of the properties of water, for example: water takes the shape of its container; water flows until it reaches a common level; some objects float in water, others sink; some substances dissolve in water; water evaporates; heating and cooling causes water to change.
- To show that the force of water can move things.
- To show that the surface of water has a tension.
- To demonstrate that water pressure increases with depth.
- To demonstrate that plants need water.
- To raise awareness of the different forms of water in a variety of weather conditions.
- To show where water in the tap comes from.
- To introduce the idea of the water cycle.
- To demonstrate that water can be cleaned.

Safety precautions

The activities described on the worksheets mainly use everyday items of equipment and materials which are perfectly safe if used sensibly. Where extra care is necessary on safety grounds, this is mentioned both on the worksheets and also in the appropriate section of the teachers' notes.

Scientific background

This information is intended to help you to understand the scientific concepts covered in this book. It goes beyond the level of understanding expected of most children, but it will give you the confidence to ask and answer questions and to guide the children in their investigations. Further information is contained in the worksheet notes.

Water

Water is a compound made of the gases hydrogen and oxygen. It is the most common substance on Earth, covering about 70 per cent of its surface. The heat from the Sun causes water to evaporate into the air, both from wet surfaces such as oceans, seas, rivers and puddles, and from trees and other plants. The water rises as vapour. As it cools, it condenses, forming tiny droplets of water which are seen as clouds. The clouds are carried along in currents of air. Rain falls when the droplets cool and join together to form larger drops. If the air is very cold, the rain may fall as snow, hail or sleet. When the water falls, it soaks through the soil and rock, forming springs, or drains into streams. The springs and streams merge, forming rivers which flow back to the sea and the oceans. This process is called the water cycle.

Water boils at 100°C, forming water vapour. We see steam when droplets form as the water vapour condenses. Water freezes at 0°C, forming ice. Ice floats as it is less dense than water.

Water is essential for all living things. Living things are made up of large amounts of water. The human body is roughly 70 per cent water.

▲ ESSENTIALS FOR SCIENCE: Water

The surface tension of water draws water inwards so that when drops are formed, they are rounded. Water flows from a tap in a rounded stream. The surface tension causes some objects that would otherwise sink to stay on the surface.

Notes on individual activities

Page 5: What is water like?
Key idea: clean tap water is colourless, does not smell and has no taste. It feels 'wet'.
Extension activity: let the children collect rainwater or river-water to compare different sources of water. **Safety precautions:** do not let them taste rain- or river-water and remind them to wash their hands after touching the water.

Page 6: What do we use water for?
Key idea: water is necessary for us to live. We use water in many ways.
Developing the investigation: discuss with the children the ways in which we use water during the day. Let them discuss the pictures and encourage them to add their own ideas. The children can go on to contribute to a class frieze showing the ways water is used in school.

Page 7: What shape is water?
Key idea: water is a liquid. It takes the shape of whatever contains it.
Developing the investigation: ask the children to make a collection of different containers, e.g., a twisty drinking straw or a plastic container with a hollow handle, and fill them with water.

Page 8: Running water
Key idea: water flows to find its own level.
Likely outcome: water running down a slope will form a narrow stream. Water on a flat surface will form a puddle.
Developing the investigation: ask the children to observe what happens when there is something in the path of water. Show pictures of rivers, lakes and the sea. Discuss how the water is moving. Have the children experienced flooding? Why does a river flood?

Page 9: Water level
Key idea: water finds its own level.
Likely outcome: water in the tubing will always be at the same level on each side because water will always be at the lowest level possible.
Extension activity: explain how water runs out of a tap. At home, water is stored in a tank which is above the level of the taps.

Page 10: Make a siphon
Key idea: air pressure on the surface of water forces the water to move up the pipe.
Likely outcome: water will flow through the tube until the water levels are the same in both bowls. (Make sure there are no air bubbles left in the tube when it is pushed under water.)
Extension activities: let the children find out what happens if the end of the tube in the lower bowl is raised. How high can the tube be raised between the bowls – does the water continue to flow through? Discuss how the air is pushing down on the surface of water in the higher bowl.

Page 11: Water surface
Key idea: surface tension provides enough force to prevent the water from overflowing.
Likely outcome: children will be able to see the curved edge of the water as they drop the counters in.
Developing the investigation: discuss how the surface of water can support some pond animals such as pond skaters.

Page 12: A drop of water
Key idea: water surface tension holds the drop of water in a curved shape. A drop of water can act as a magnifier.
Likely outcome: children will see the curved edge of a drop of water and find out how many drops they can add to the original drop before the surface tension breaks and the water flows.

Page 13: Drops of water on surfaces
Key idea: some materials absorb water, others do not.
Likely outcome: foil, plastic and waxed paper will not absorb water. Other materials will.
Developing the investigation: discuss the word 'absorb' and 'absorbtion'. Talk about things used to absorb water, e.g., sponges and paper towels.

Page 14: Washing hands
Key idea: we use water for washing. Warm water and soap make washing more effective.
Extension activity: let the children make the same investigation using different substances to make 'dirty' hands such as paint or newsprint.

Page 15: Puddle puzzle
Key idea: water evaporates.
Extension activity: give the children two containers such as a bowl and a plastic bottle. Let them monitor evaporation over time.

Page 16: Water disappears into the air
Key idea: water evaporates into the air.
Likely outcome: the beaker of water with the plastic cover will weigh more because the plastic film will prevent the water vapour from escaping into the air.
Developing the investigation: discuss with the

▲ ESSENTIALS FOR SCIENCE: Water

children how water seems to disappear as things dry. Explain the word 'evaporate'. Water is in the air as a vapour which we cannot see.

Page 17: The best weather for drying

Key idea: the weather affects how quickly water evaporates.
Likely outcome: more water will have evaporated in sunny, windy weather.
Developing the investigation: ask the children what has happened to the water. Do they think large amounts of water evaporate from the sea?

Page 18: From steam to water

Key idea: steam is tiny droplets of water in the air. When steam touches something cold it condenses and becomes water.
Likely outcome: when steam touches the ladle it will mist up the surface and then form drops of water.
Extension activity: discuss the different types of machines which use steam power.
Safety precautions: when working with hot water, children should be supervised at all times.

Page 19: Where does water come from?

Key idea: the water in our taps is part of the water cycle.
Developing the investigation: discuss how water evaporates, especially when the sun is shining on the surface of the water, forming water vapour which we cannot see. The air cools, droplets form and join, forming larger drops which fall as rain. Rain eventually flows into rivers.

Page 20: Make a rain gauge

Key idea: water falls as rain. Rainfall can be measured over a period of time.
Developing the investigation: discuss weather and weather forecasting with the children. Let them look out for rain clouds.

Page 21: Keeping ice cubes cold

Key idea: insulators such as woollen fabric, newspaper or polystyrene can help to keep substances cool.
Likely outcome: the unwrapped ice cube will melt first.
Developing the investigation: discuss how we keep things cool. When we go on a picnic we use a cool box. What is the cool box lined with? (Frequently it is expanded polystyrene.)

Page 22: An ice cube melting

Key idea: ice is frozen water. When ice is warmed it becomes water again. Some substances such as salt speed the melting.
Likely outcome: the ice will slowly melt. Remind the children to look at the melting ice at intervals.
Developing the investigation: talk about freezing water with the children. Where do we freeze water? Let them feel an ice cube and look at it with a hand lens.

Page 23: Dissolving things in water

Key idea: some substances dissolve in water. Others sink to the bottom.
Developing the investigation: discuss what we mean by the word 'dissolve'. Put a teaspoon of instant coffee into hot water. Let the children see what happens. Decide with the children whether each beaker will be stirred.

Page 24: Dilute a drink

Key idea: water can be added to dilute a solution.
Likely outcome: the taste and colour will change as more water is added.
Developing the investigation: discuss the words 'dilute' and 'concentrated' with the children. Which drinks do they have at home which need to be diluted?

Page 25: Floating and sinking

Key idea: some objects float in water, others sink.
Developing the investigation: test out further ideas, such as do all wooden things float or do all glass things sink? Do some things which are empty float and some things which are full of water sink? Can the children make any of the floaters sink or sinkers float?

Page 26: Pushing water

Key idea: water exerts an upward pressure, or upthrust, on floating objects, and this can be felt. Floating objects displace water.
Likely outcome: the harder the floating ball is pressed down into the water, the harder the water seems to be pushing upwards. Each ball displaces its own weight of water, and this causes the water level in the bucket to rise.
Extension activities: discuss the use of lifebuoys, inflatable arm-bands and life-jackets.

Page 27: Jugs of water

Key idea: water presses down. The pressure increases with the depth of water.
Likely outcome: the water jet from the bottle with the hole near the base has more force because of the greater pressure from the weight of water.
Extension activity: let the children make two or three holes in a line down another squeezy bottle. Ask them how the water will jet out of the holes. Let them find out.

Page 28: Do seeds need water to grow?

Key idea: seeds need water to grow.
Likely outcome: the seeds in the beaker containing water will germinate. The others will not.

▲ ESSENTIALS FOR SCIENCE: Water

Developing the investigation: discuss what seeds and plants need to grow. Let the children continue to grow the seeds.

Page 29: Do plants take up water?

Key idea: plants take up water through their stems.
Likely outcome: the coloured water will be visible in the celery stem. The flower may change to the colour of the water.
Developing the investigation: discuss what plants need to live. Ask how the children think the water gets into the plant.

Page 30: What did I drink today?

Key idea: we need water to stay healthy. Things we drink and many things we eat contain large amounts of water.
Developing the investigation: ask the children to compare the records they make. Ask them how they could find out how much they drink in a day.

Page 31: Making a water filter

Key idea: filtering water helps to purify it.
Likely outcome: the water will be visibly cleaner after it has passed through the filter.
Developing the investigation: discuss with the children how water is pumped from rivers and reservoirs to the waterworks. At the waterworks the water is cleaned in a series of processes including a filter bed. Send for information from your local water board.

Page 32: Water in our homes

Key idea: clean water is piped to our homes from the water mains and used water is piped away through waste pipes to the sewer.
Developing the investigation: take the children to see the water mains in the school and discover where the waste pipes go to the main sewer. Take the children to a sewage plant if possible.
Extension activity: ask the children how they could save water.

National Curriculum: Science

In addition to the PoS for AT1, these pages support the following requirements of the National Curriculum for Science.

AT2 – Pupils should:
• investigate what plants need to grow and reproduce;
• take responsibility for the care of living things, maintaining their welfare by knowing about their needs and understanding the care required.

AT3 – Pupils should:
• collect and find similarities and differences between a variety of everyday materials. These should include natural and manufactured materials such as (...) water (...). They should explore the properties of these materials referring, for example, to their shape, colour and texture, and consider some of their everyday uses. They should see how some can be changed by simple processes such as dissolving, pouring;
• develop an awareness of which materials they are using are naturally occurring and which are manufactured. They should explore the effects of heating some everyday substances, for example, ice (and) water (...) in order to understand how heating and cooling bring about melting and solidifying;
• observe the effects of weathering in their locality.

AT4 – Pupils should:
• talk about when and why they feel hot or cold and link the sensations of hot and cold with thermometer measurements, for example in water;
• have early experiences of devices which move. They should experience the natural force of gravity pulling things down and manufactured forces (...). These forces should be experienced in the way they push, pull, make things move, stop things and change the shape of objects (...). They should explore floating and sinking and relate their experiences to water safety;
• observe closely the local natural environment to detect seasonal changes including weather.

Scottish 5-14 Curriculum: Environmental studies

Attainment outcomes	Strands
Science in the environment	Processes of life; energy; forces; materials; planet earth; weather and climate
Living with technology	Technology and needs; technology, design and control
Healthy and safe living	Looking after myself; my environment
Investigating	Planning; finding out; recording; interpreting; reporting
Positive attitudes to the environment	Conservation and avoiding waste

▲ ESSENTIALS FOR SCIENCE: Water

▲ Name _____

What is water like?

You will need: a beaker of clean water from the tap.

▲ How many things can you find out about water, using your senses?

What does water look like?

Can you see through the clean water?

Does water smell?

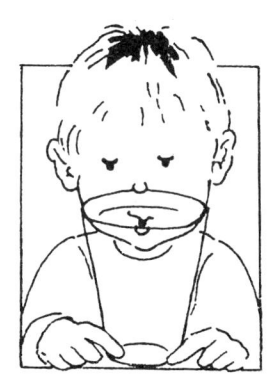

Has it a taste?

What does water feel like?

Does still water make a sound?

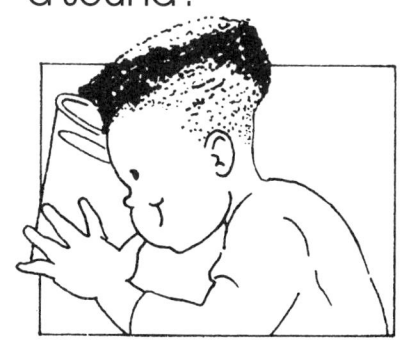

▲ Dip your fingers in the water and let the drops fall back into the water. Do the drops make a sound?

▲ Is there anything else you can find out about water using your senses?

▲ ESSENTIALS FOR SCIENCE: Water

▲ Name _____

What do we use water for?

▲ Colour the parts of the picture that show how we use water.

▲ Think of other ways in which water is used. Add your own pictures or make a list on the back of this sheet.

▲ ESSENTIALS FOR SCIENCE: Water

6

▲ Name _____

What shape is water?

You will need: a jug of water; other containers of different shapes.

▲ What shape is the water in the jug?

▲ Pour the water into another container. What shape is the water now?

▲ What shape will the water be when you pour it into other containers?

▲ What does this tell you about the shape of water?

▲ Draw the containers and water below.

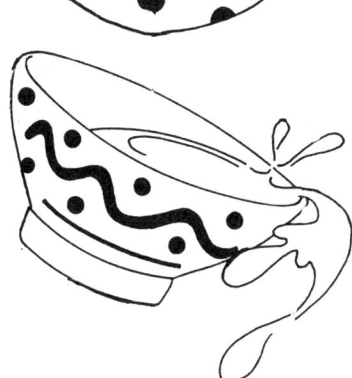

▲ ESSENTIALS FOR SCIENCE: Water

▲ Name _____

Running water

You will need: jugs of water; a plastic tray or a piece of guttering.

▲ Make a slope with the plastic tray or the piece of guttering.

▲ If you pour water gently, which way do you think it will run? Pour the water slowly and watch.

▲ Will water move in the same way on a flat surface?

▲ Lay the tray or guttering flat and try it. Did the water run where you expected?

▲ In the space below, draw the pathway of the water on the sloping and the flat surface.

▲ What have you found out about water?

On the slope	On flat ground

▲ ESSENTIALS FOR SCIENCE: Water

▲ Name _____

Water level

You will need: a length of clear tubing; a funnel; a jug of water.

Work with a partner.

▲ Push the end of the funnel into one end of the tubing.

▲ Ask a friend to pour water into the funnel while you hold the tubing in a U shape.

▲ What do you notice about the water levels on either side of the tubing?

▲ Raise one side of the tubing and then lower it. What do you notice about the water level?

▲ In the tube below, draw in the water level.

▲ Add your own drawings of ways you changed the shape of the tubing. Put the water levels in your drawings.

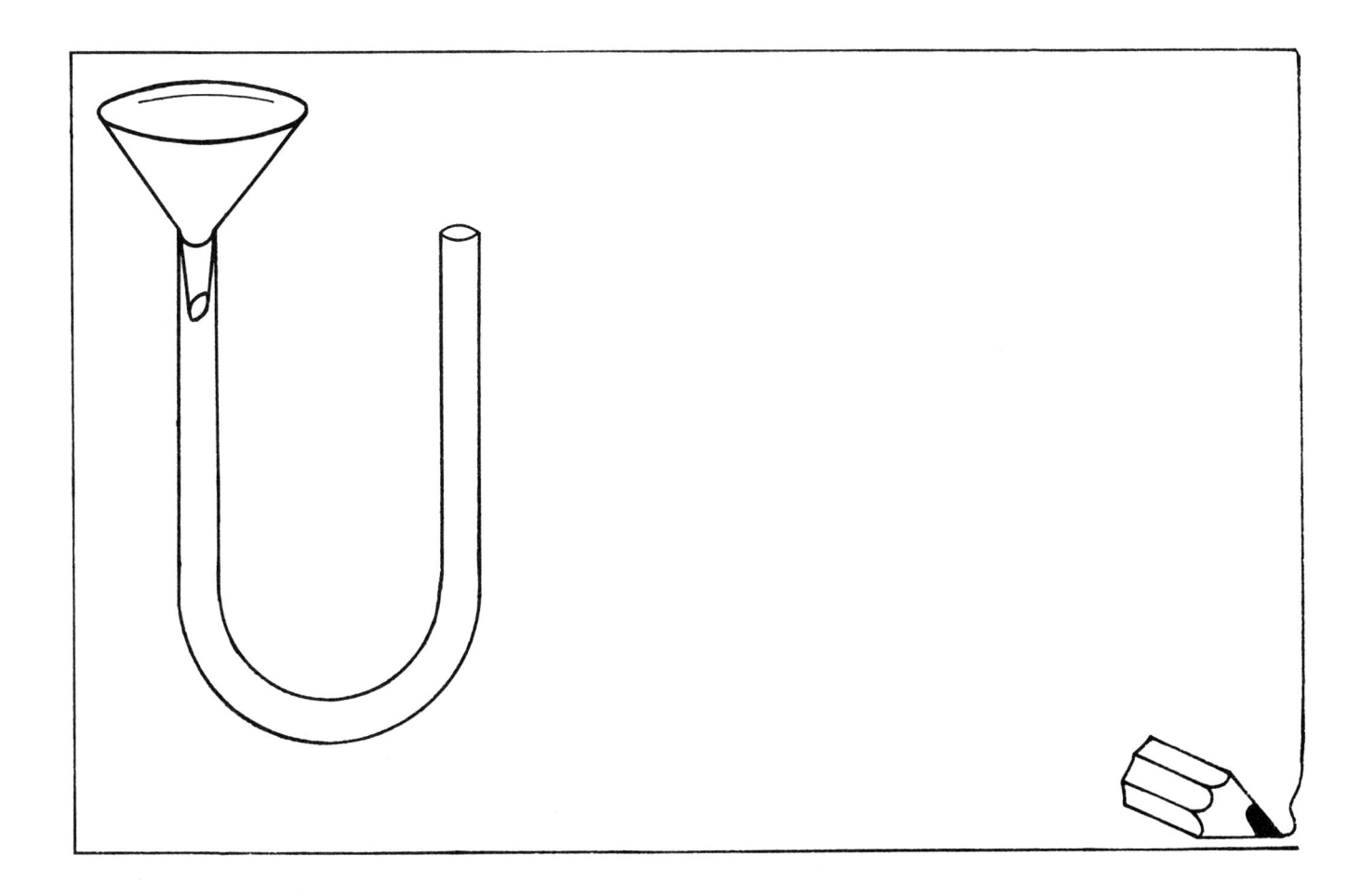

▲ ESSENTIALS FOR SCIENCE: Water

▲ Name _____

Make a siphon

You will need: two bowls; a length of tubing; water.

Work with a friend.

▲ Fill one bowl with water and place it higher than the second bowl.

▲ Push one end of the tubing under the water in the higher bowl.

▲ Fill the tubing with water but keep your thumb over the end so that it doesn't pour out.

▲ Place the end with your thumb over it in the lower bowl. Release your thumb.

▲ You have made a siphon. What is pushing the water along the tube?

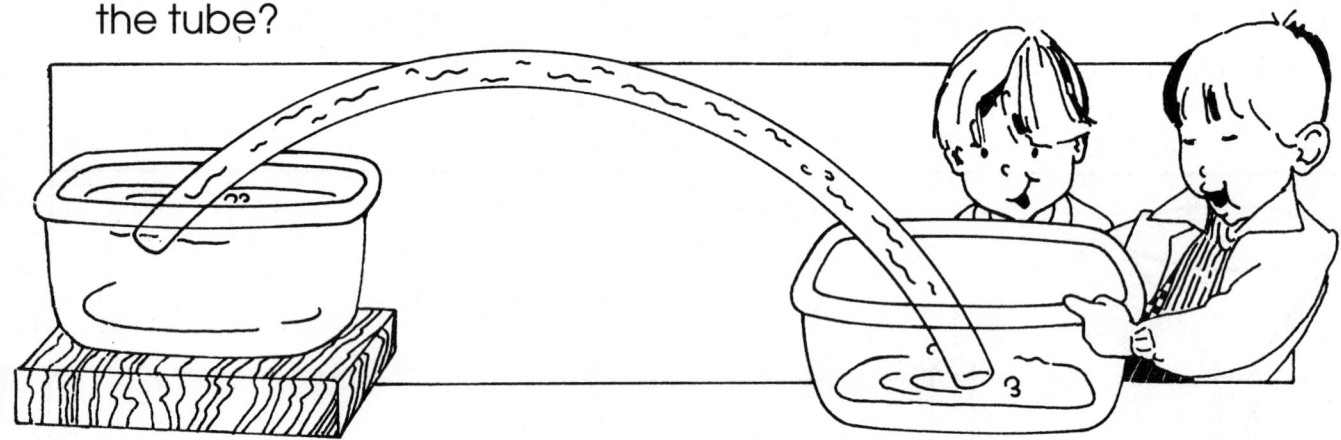

▲ Draw the levels of water in the picture below to show what happens.

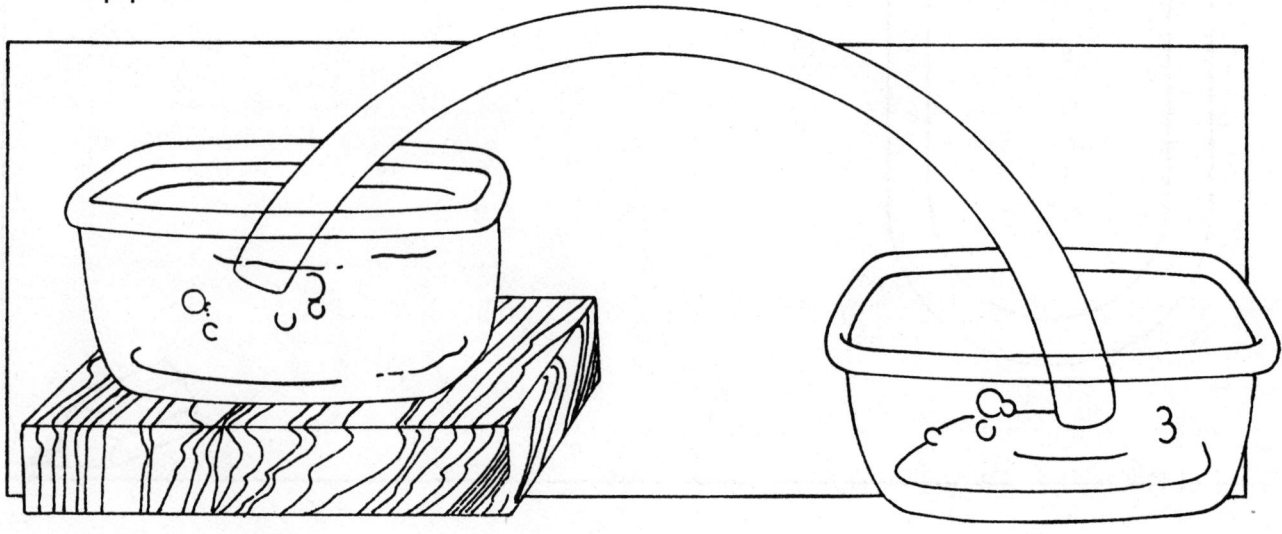

▲ ESSENTIALS FOR SCIENCE: Water

▲ Name _____

Water surface

You will need: a clear beaker; water; plastic counters.

▲ Fill the beaker to the brim with water.

▲ Look at the surface of the water.

▲ Slip counters into the water.

▲ Watch what happens to the surface of the water.

▲ Add more counters.

▲ Watch how the surface of the water curves up above the rim of the beaker.

▲ How many counters can you put in the glass before it overflows?

▲ The surface of water can hold up things which would otherwise sink.

▲ Lay a small plastic counter on the surface of the water. Can you make it stay there?

▲ ESSENTIALS FOR SCIENCE: Water

A drop of water

You will need: a plastic dropper; a beaker of water; a clear plastic lid (Petri dish); a hand lens.

▲ Learn how to use the dropper. Then put one drop of water on the plastic lid.

▲ Use the hand lens to look closely at the water.

▲ Add two more drops and look closely again. Can you see the curved edge of the blob of water?

▲ How many drops do you need to add to the blob before it overflows and changes shape?

▲ Draw and write about what you saw.

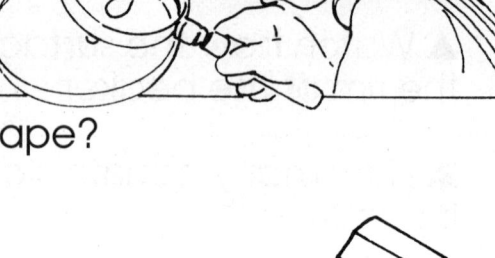

1 drop	3 drops	More drops

▲ Lift up the lid and hold it over some writing. What do you notice about the writing when you look through the water?

▲ What else can you find out about a drop of water?

▲ ESSENTIALS FOR SCIENCE: Water

▲ Name _____

Drops of water on surfaces

You will need: a plastic dropper; a hand lens; a jug of water; glue; small pieces of each of the following: foil, plastic bag, waxed paper, kitchen roll, newspaper, art paper.

Work with a friend.

▲ Drop one or two drops of water on each material. What happens?

▲ Use a hand lens to see clearly. Which materials soak up water?

▲ Divide the materials into two sets and list them on the chart below.

These absorbed water	These did not absorb water

▲ Find some more materials to test. Add them to the chart.

▲ ESSENTIALS FOR SCIENCE: Water

▲ Name _____

Washing hands

You will need: cold water; hand-hot water; soap; paper towels; a clock timer.

Work with two friends.

▲ One person will be the time-keeper. The other two should make their hands muddy.

▲ Now one person should get ready to wash their hands in cold water and the other in hot water.

▲ Start the timer. Wash the hands for half a minute. Whose hands are the cleanest?

▲ Now try again using soap as well for half a minute.

▲ What have you found out? Draw and write about it in the spaces below.

Cold water

Hot water

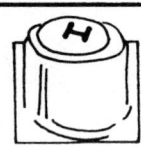

Cold water and soap

Hot water and soap

▲ What would happen if you washed your hands in coloured water?

▲ ESSENTIALS FOR SCIENCE: Water

▲ Name _____

Puddle puzzle

You will need: a jug of water; a plastic sheet; chalk; a felt-tipped pen.

Work with a friend. Choose a sunny day.

▲ After it has rained, make a chalk mark round the edge of a puddle.

▲ Draw round it again later.
  • Has the size of the puddle changed?
  • Where has the water gone?
  • Could the water have gone into the ground?

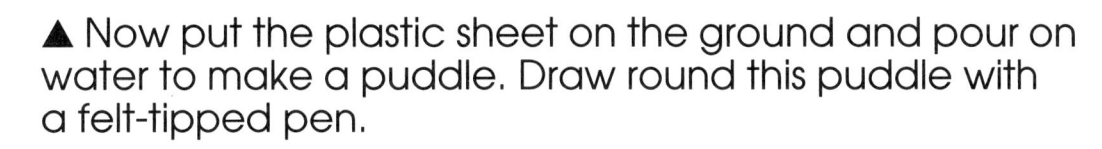

▲ Now put the plastic sheet on the ground and pour on water to make a puddle. Draw round this puddle with a felt-tipped pen.

▲ Draw round it again later.
  • Has the size of the puddle changed?
  • Where has the water gone?

▲ Draw and write about it below.

▲ Draw your puddle with the chalk marks to show how the puddle has changed.

▲ ESSENTIALS FOR SCIENCE: Water

▲ Name _____

Water disappears into the air

You will need: balance scales; two clear plastic beakers; a dropper; plastic film.

Work with a friend.

▲ Pour exactly the same amount of water into the two beakers.

▲ Put them on the balance scales and add drops of water to the lighter beaker until they balance.

▲ Now cover one of the beakers with plastic film.

▲ Leave the beakers on the balance scales for a day. Do the beakers still weigh the same?

▲ What has happened to the water in the lighter beaker?

▲ Draw the balance scales and beakers on the first day and on the second day.

day 1	day 2

▲ Find out what happens if you leave the beakers for several days.

▲ ESSENTIALS FOR SCIENCE: Water

▲ Name _____

The best weather for drying

You will need: two plates; a measuring jug.

Work with a friend.

▲ Put one plate in a sunny spot outside and the other in a shady spot outside.

▲ Pour the same amount of water on to each plate. Mark the level of the water.

▲ Leave for a few hours and then check what has happened.

▲ What did you find out? Write and draw about it below.

In the sun 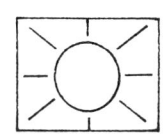   **In the shade**

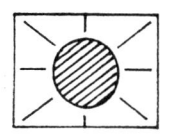

▲ Try the same experiment on a windy day. Put one plate in an exposed position and the other in a sheltered position. Record what happened below.

In the wind    **Out of the wind**

▲ ESSENTIALS FOR SCIENCE: Water

▲ Name _____

From steam to water   ⚠️

You will need: a kettle of boiling water; a ladle or a tablespoon.

Ask an adult to carry out this experiment.

▲ What is steam? Watch the steam rising from a boiling kettle. **Steam is hot. Do not try to touch it.**

▲ Ask an adult to hold a ladle or a spoon against the steam. What happens?

▲ Hold the ladle away from the kettle. When it is cold touch it.
- What can you see and feel?
- What has happened to the steam?

▲ In the space below, draw and label what happened to the steam when it touched the ladle.

The steam changed into water on the ladle.

▲ Could you turn the water into steam again?

▲ ESSENTIALS FOR SCIENCE: Water

▲ Name _____

Where does water come from?

Work with your friends.

▲ Look at the picture below. Talk about what is in the picture.

▲ Colour in the sun and the water.

▲ Put arrows to show which way the water is moving. Which way will the arrows point when the sun is shining on the water?

▲ Follow the water cycle to find out how the water gets to your taps.

▲ Do you think the same water is used over and over again?

▲ ESSENTIALS FOR SCIENCE: Water   19

▲ Name _____

Make a rain gauge

You will need: a clear plastic bottle; scissors.

Ask an adult to help.

▲ Cut off the top section of the plastic bottle.

▲ Turn it upside down and put it in the base.

▲ Stand the rain gauge in open ground.

▲ Each day check how much water has collected in the rain gauge.

▲ Keep a record for a week.

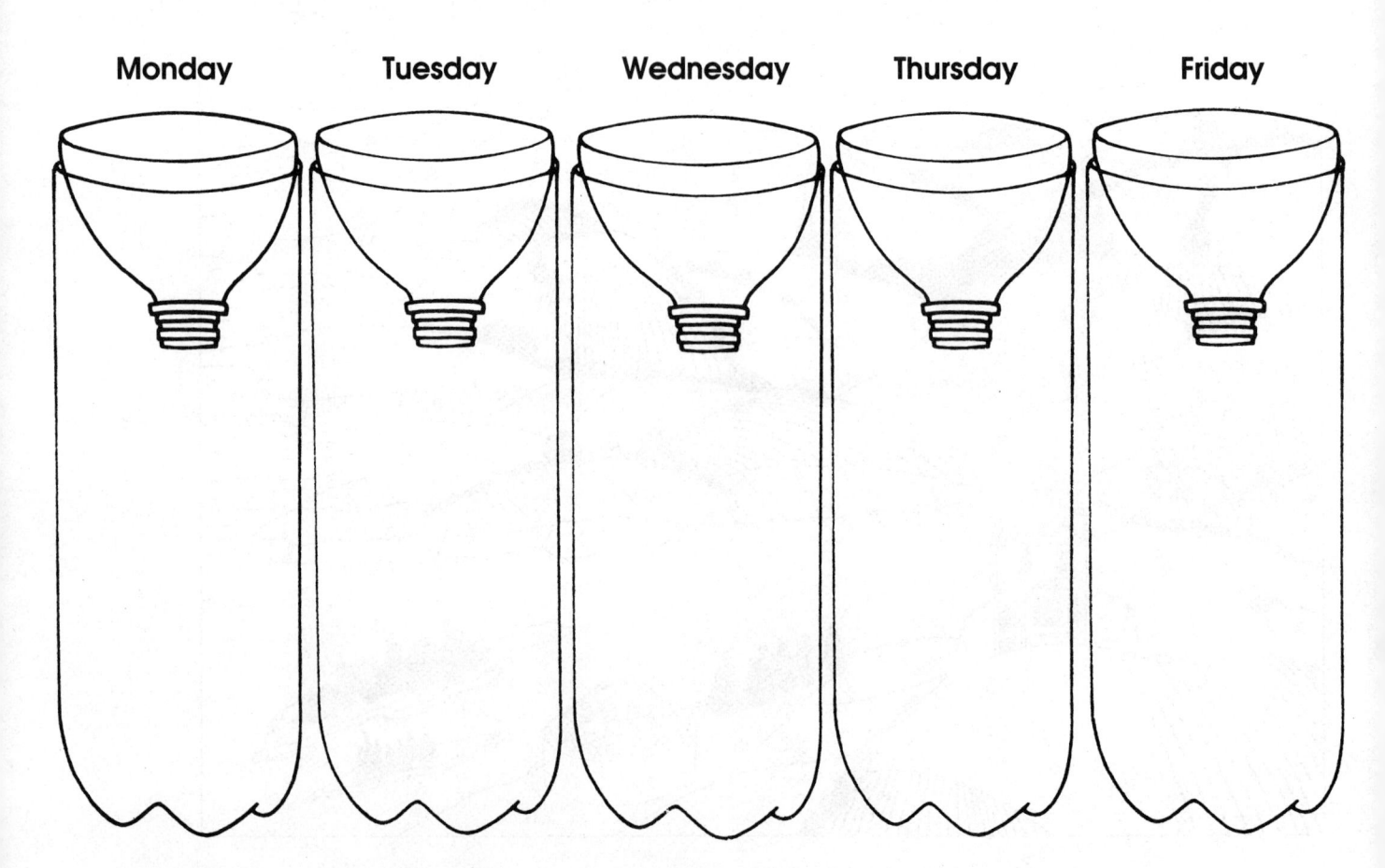

| Monday | Tuesday | Wednesday | Thursday | Friday |

▲ How much rain fell in the week?

▲ Compare this rainfall with the weekly rainfall during another season of the year.

▲ ESSENTIALS FOR SCIENCE: Water

▲ Name _____

Keeping cold

You will need: four small plastic bags; ice cubes; a collection of materials to wrap the bags in, for example, a woollen blanket, newspaper, foil, pieces of polythene; a timer.

Work with a friend.

Who can make an ice cube last the longest?

▲ Put one ice cube in each plastic bag.

▲ Put a different material round three of the bags. Do not put anything around the fourth bag.

▲ Put all the bags in the same place. Leave them for 15 minutes.

▲ Which bag kept the ice cubes the coolest?

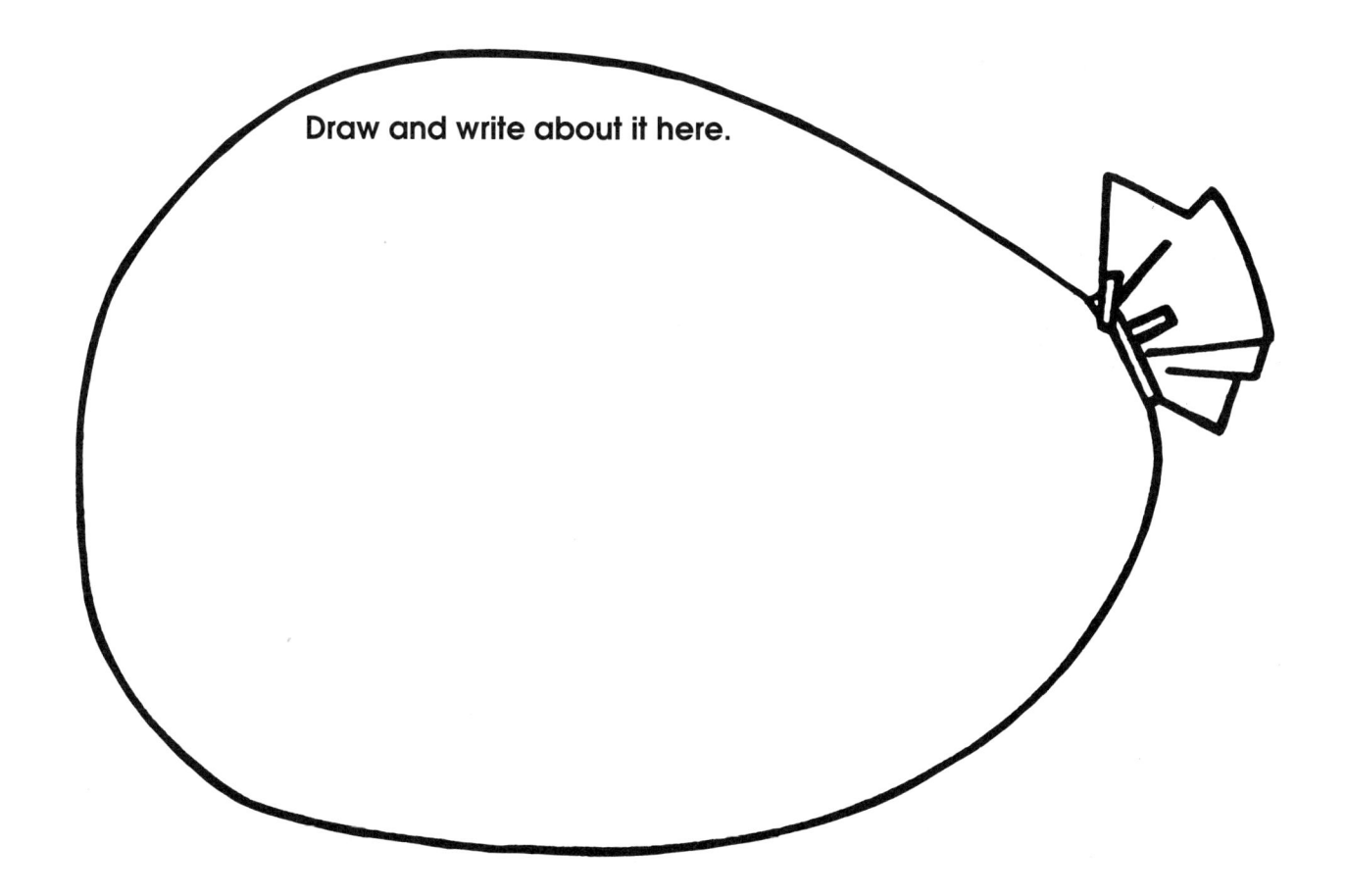

Draw and write about it here.

▲ How do you keep food cool when you go on a picnic?

▲ ESSENTIALS FOR SCIENCE: Water

▲ Name _____

An ice cube melting

You will need: ice cubes; warm water; salt; a mixture of salt and sand; small bowls; a timer.

▲ Put an ice cube on a saucer in a warm place. Look at it every few minutes. How long did it take to melt?

▲ How do you think you could melt an ice cube quickly? Try out your own ideas.

▲ Put an ice cube in each of the four bowls.

▲ Add warm water to one, salt to another, a mixture of sand and salt to another and nothing to the fourth.

▲ Put on the timer. How long does each ice cube take to melt? Which melts the quickest?

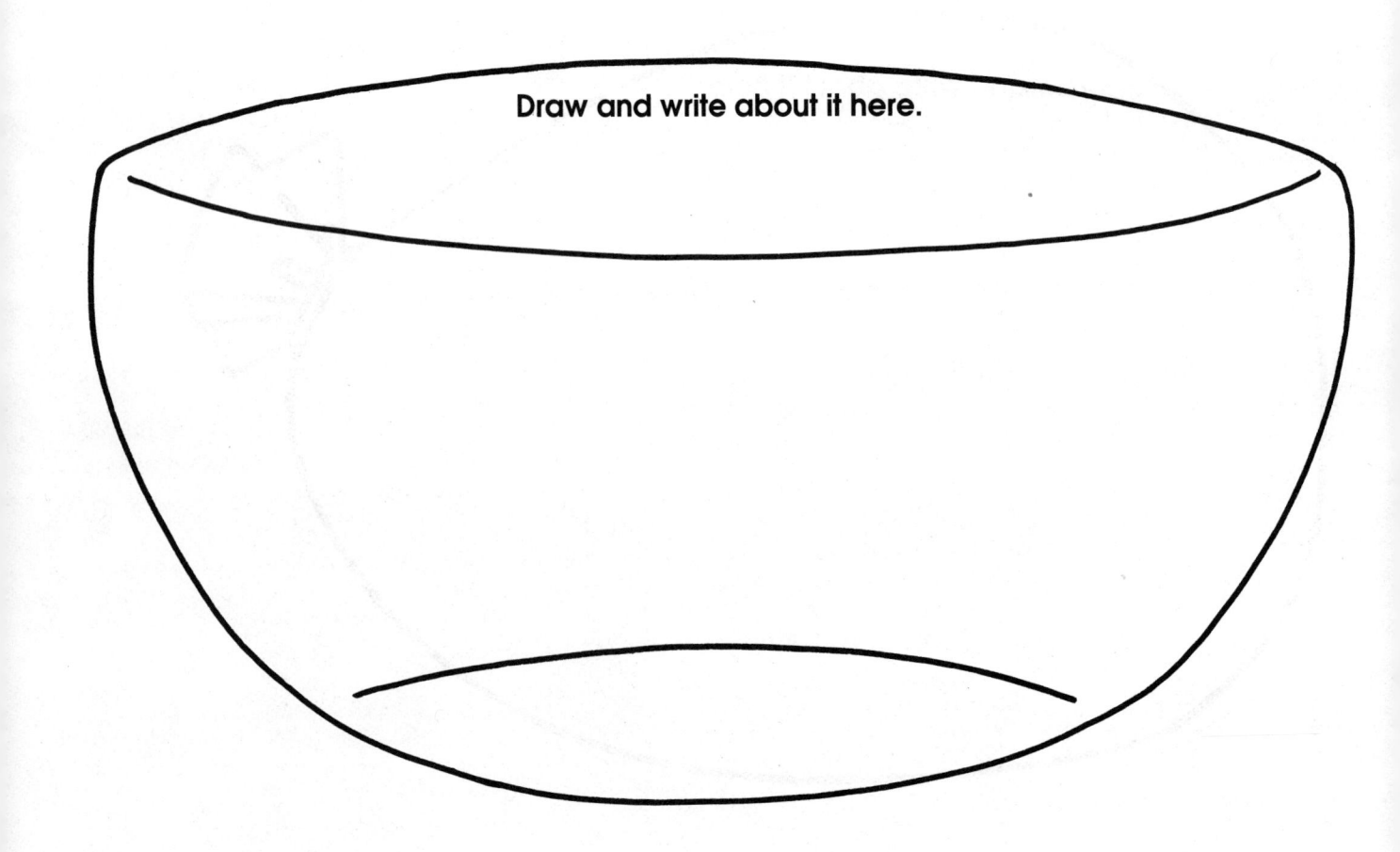

Draw and write about it here.

▲ ESSENTIALS FOR SCIENCE: Water

▲ Name _____

Dissolving things in water

You will need: clear plastic beakers; a spoonful of some of the following: salt, sugar, soil, sand, clay, custard powder, flour, bicarbonate of soda, rice, cocoa.

Work with a friend.

▲ Put a spoonful of each substance in a beaker of water.

▲ Look closely at what happens.

▲ Leave them for a day.

▲ The next day, look again and record what happened.

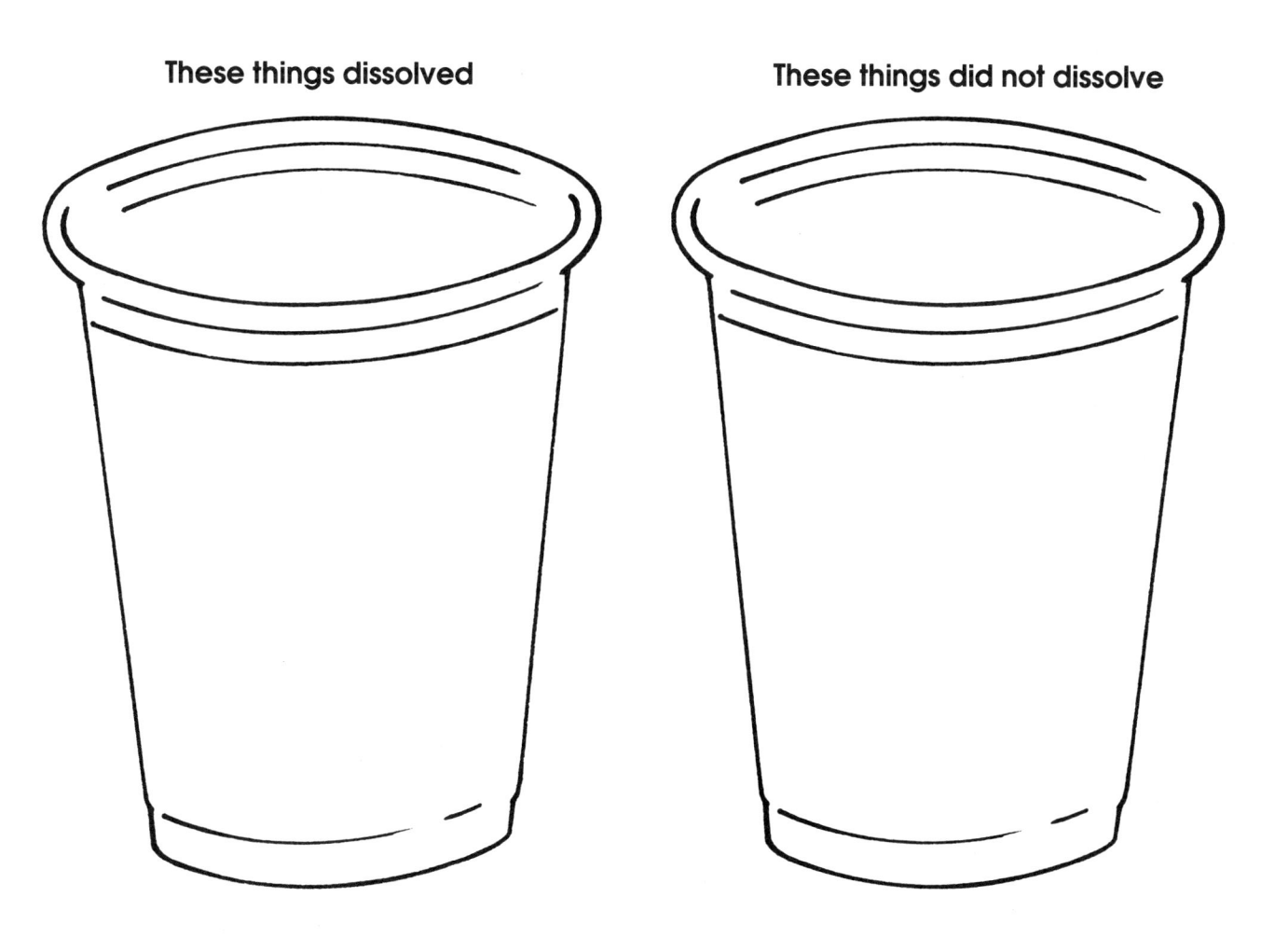

These things dissolved

These things did not dissolve

▲ ESSENTIALS FOR SCIENCE: Water

▲ Name _____

Dilute a drink

You will need: a liquid measure (you could use a large spoon or an egg-cup); concentrated orange juice; a jug of water; clear plastic beakers.

▲ Pour a measure of concentrated orange juice into a beaker. What does it look like? How does it taste?

▲ Pour a measure of juice and a measure of water into the next beaker. What changes do you notice?

▲ Pour one measure of juice and two measures of water into the next beaker. Check the taste and colour.

▲ Add measures of water until you have found the mixture you like best. How many measures of water to one measure of juice did it need?

▲ Draw and label what you did.

▲ Are there any other concentrated-drink flavours you could try?

▲ ESSENTIALS FOR SCIENCE: Water

▲ Name _____

Floating and sinking

You will need: a collection of different objects; a jug of water; paper towels.

▲ Put the objects in water one at a time.

▲ Find out which ones float and which ones sink.

▲ Draw and label the objects to make a set of things which float and a set of things which sink.

These float

These sink

▲ What kinds of things float?

▲ What kinds of things sink?

▲ ESSENTIALS FOR SCIENCE: Water

▲ Name _____

Pushing water

You will need: a small ball; a large ball; a bucket half-filled with water; a pencil.

▲ Mark the level of water in the bucket.

▲ Float the small ball in the water.

▲ Push the ball under the water. What do you feel?

▲ What happens to the water level in the bucket?

▲ Now float the large ball in the bucket.

▲ Push the ball under the water. What do you feel?

▲ What happens to the water level in the bucket?

▲ Which ball did you have to push the hardest to make it go under the water?

▲ Which ball made the water level in the bucket change the most?

▲ ESSENTIALS FOR SCIENCE: Water

▲ Name _____

Jets of water

You will need: two plastic squeezy bottles; masking tape; scissors; a large nail; a hammer.

Ask an adult to help you.

▲ Use the nail to make a hole near the base in one bottle and near the top in the other.

▲ Seal the holes with masking tape.

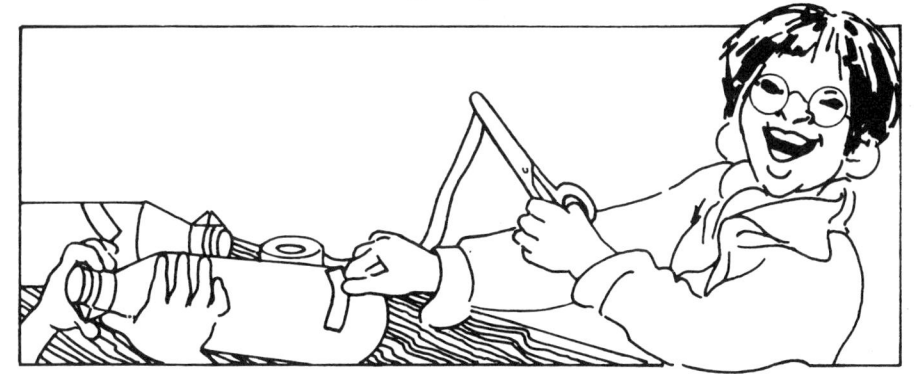

▲ Fill the bottles with water and stand them outside.

▲ Peel off the masking tape from one bottle. What happens?

▲ Peel off the masking tape from the other. Does the same thing happen?

▲ On the bottles below draw how the water came out of the two holes.

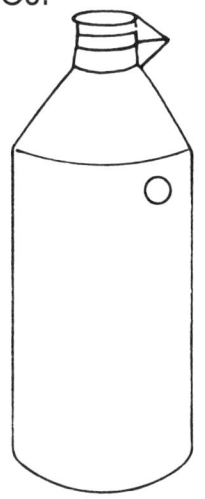

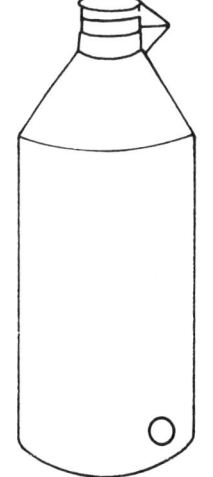

▲ Why were the jets of water different?

▲ What happens if you put a hole in the middle of the bottle?

▲ ESSENTIALS FOR SCIENCE: Water

▲ Name _____

Does water help things to grow?

You will need: seeds such as nasturtiums, peas or cress; two small jars filled with soil; plastic film.

▲ Put some seeds on the soil in both beakers.

▲ Water the soil in one of the beakers.

▲ Put plastic film over each beaker and place them in good light, but not direct sunlight.

▲ What do you think will happen?

▲ Look each day.

▲ Record what happens on the drawings below.

[no water]   [water]

▲ What does this tell you about growing seeds?

▲ ESSENTIALS FOR SCIENCE: Water

▲ Name _____

Do plants take up water?

You will need: a stick of celery; a white flower such as a daisy; food colouring; a clear container; a knife.

Ask an adult to help you.

▲ Pour some water into the container.

▲ Add a few drops of food colouring.

▲ Put the stick of celery in the water.

▲ Put the container in a warm place. Leave it for about an hour.

▲ Now cut across the stem of the celery stick. What do you see?

▲ Cut across the stem in other places.

▲ Try the same thing using the white flower.

▲ What have you found out? Draw and write about it here.

▲ ESSENTIALS FOR SCIENCE: Water

▲ Name _____

What did you drink today?

We need to drink water to stay healthy. The liquids we drink contain large amounts of water.

▲ Look at the pictures below.

▲ Colour the pictures of things you like to eat or drink.

▲ Add your own ideas on the back of this sheet.

▲ Make a record of all the drink you have in one day.

Morning	Afternoon	Evening

▲ Can you find out about how many litres this adds up to?

▲ ESSENTIALS FOR SCIENCE: Water

▲ Name _____

Make a water filter

You will need: a jug of water; a spoonful of garden soil; a flowerpot; some gravel or small stones; sand; a coffee filter paper or kitchen roll; a clear beaker; cotton wool.

Work with a friend.

▲ Stir the garden soil into the jug of water.

▲ Make a filter like this:

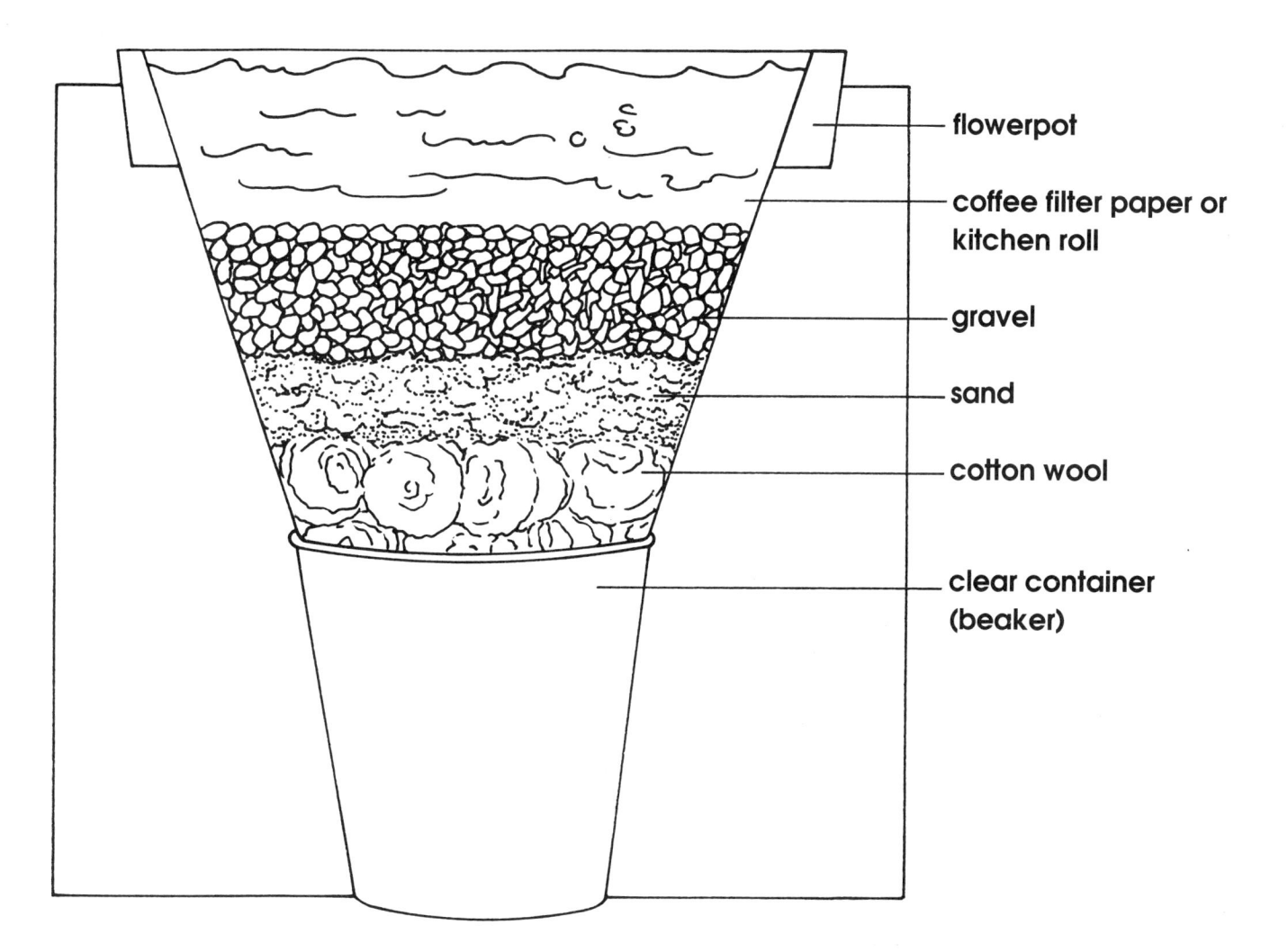

- flowerpot
- coffee filter paper or kitchen roll
- gravel
- sand
- cotton wool
- clear container (beaker)

▲ Pour the muddy water slowly through the filter.

▲ What does the water look like now?

Remember that the water is not clean enough to drink or use for washing.

▲ ESSENTIALS FOR SCIENCE: Water

▲ Name _____

Water in our homes

Work with a friend.

▲ Look at the picture below.

▲ Imagine that water is blue. Colour in blue all the water in the pipes and where water is being used in the home.

▲ Colour the used water grey.

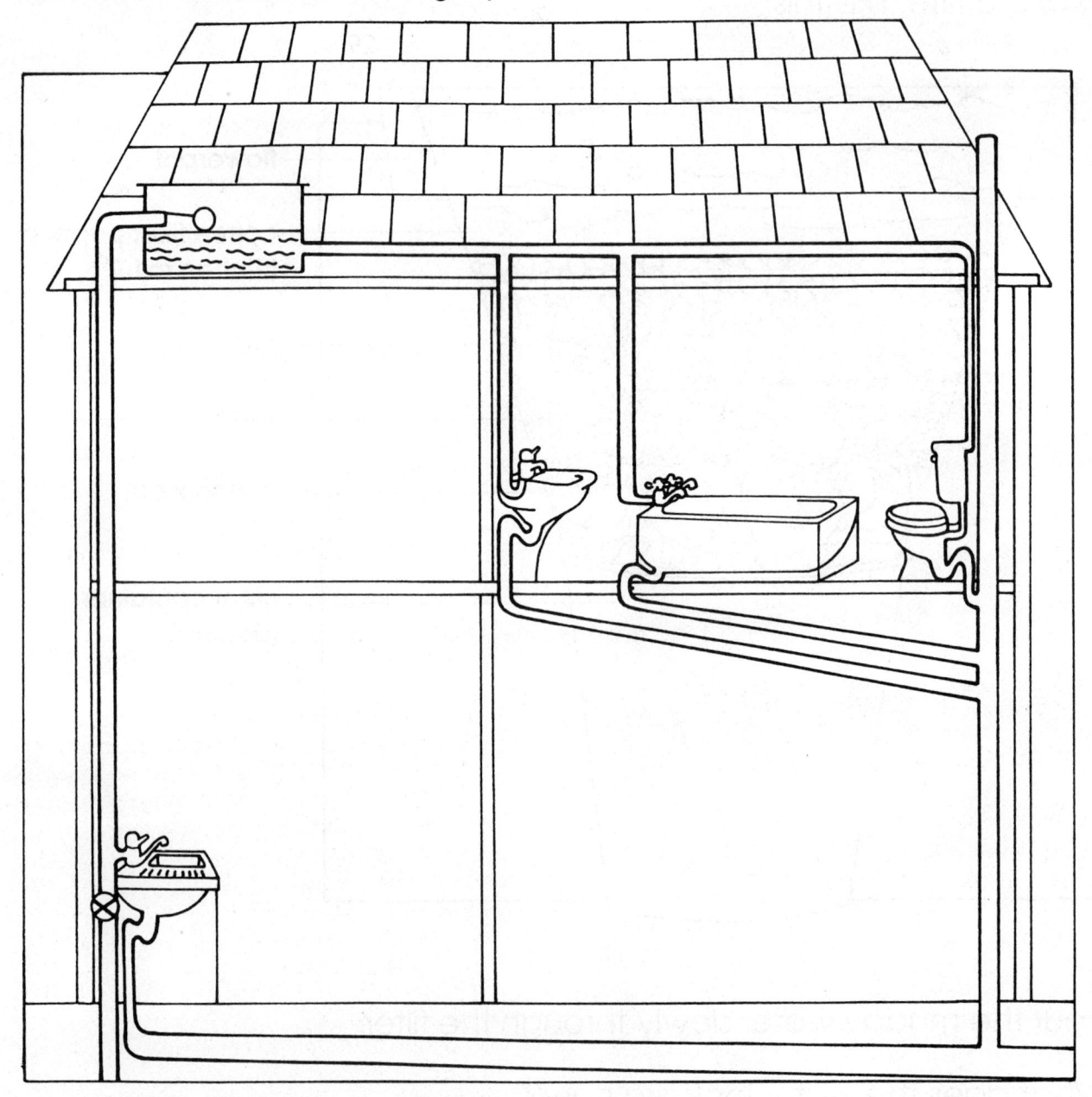

▲ Find out where the clean water comes from.

▲ Find out where used water goes to.

▲ ESSENTIALS FOR SCIENCE: Water

Contents

Teachers' notes	1
Notes on individual activities	3
Fruit and seeds	5
From plant to seed	6
Food from plants	7
Fruit and vegetables	8
Fruit colours	9
Packets of seeds	10
Sorting seeds	11
Measure some seeds	12
Runner bean seeds	13
Inside a broad bean seed	14
Warmth and cold	15
Hairy clowns	16
Which way up?	17
Watch your seeds grow	18
Measure a runner bean	19
Make a runner bean maze	20
Growing acorns	21
Grow some pips and stones	22
Scattering seeds	23
Dandelion clock	24
Winged fruit	25
Seeds we eat	26
Which seeds do birds like best?	27
Garden weeds	28
Grow cuttings	29
Growing bulbs	30
The parts of a plant	31
Beans and light	32

Teachers' notes

Aims of this book
- To introduce simple ideas on the structure of plants;
- To introduce the idea that plants and plant parts provide us with food;
- To examine the differences between fruit and vegetables;
- To examine the differences between fruit and seeds;
- To show the structure of a seed;
- To show the conditions necessary for germination to occur;
- To show how and why seeds are dispersed from the parent plant;
- To show the effect of light on plant growth;
- To show the role of seeds in a plant's life cycle;
- To introduce some other methods of plant propagation besides seeds.

Developing science skills

While it is not essential to follow the order of the worksheets, it is important that all those covering one aspect of a subject, such as the effect of light on plant growth, are dealt with at approximately the same time.

Although it is in the *doing* of science that children learn best, this involves more than just practical work. As well as needing to observe, record, predict, measure, look for patterns, classify, ask questions and so on, children need time to discuss their work.

The worksheets should be discussed both before and after completion of the activity. This helps to clarify the main ideas and will help you to monitor progress and discover what interests the children, with a view to developing their interests in future sessions.

Scientific background

Dispersal
Flowering plants which reproduce sexually bear seeds. These each consist of a food store surrounding a miniature or embryo plant.

A fruit is the part of the plant which encloses the seeds. Many vegetables, such as runner beans, are really fruits.

As plants stay rooted in one place, their fruit are almost always adapted so that they disperse their seeds easily, ensuring that new plants do not take up valuable soil space that is needed by the parents. Some fruit are designed to be scattered by the wind while others are dispersed by animals. The fruit of the coconut palm and the seeds of kingcup and water lily float and are carried by water to new locations.

Germination
A seed will remain dormant until conditions are suitable for it to germinate. 'Germination' is the process in which the embryo inside the seed starts to grow. In order for this to happen, the seed needs air (or oxygen), water and warmth. A few seeds also need light, and all seedlings must have light if they are to develop green pigment (chlorophyll), and grow into healthy plants.

▲ ESSENTIALS FOR SCIENCE: Seeds and seedlings

Growth

The first part to emerge from a germinating seed is the young root (radicle), which grows down into the soil, then the young shoot (plumule) begins to grow upwards, drawing on the food store in the seed until the first leaves are formed. The shoot responds to light and grows towards it as soon as it reaches the surface.

Seeds and fruit as food

Seeds and fruit form an important part of our diet. As well as those we eat directly, for example, peas, beans, rice and apples, many other foods are made from seeds such as bread, breakfast cereals, pasta, flour, cakes and coffee.

Notes on individual activities

Safety precautions: Warn the children that some seeds and fruit are poisonous. They should be supervised at all times.

Page 5: Fruit and seeds

Key ideas: The differences between fruit and seeds, and the relationship between them.
Developing the investigation: Point out that seeds are sometimes called 'pips' or 'stones'.
Extension: Discuss the differences between fruit and vegetables.

Page 6: From plant to seed

Key ideas: All plants have flowers. Fruit and seeds develop from flowers.
Developing the investigation: Discuss what seeds develop into. For example, an acorn into an oak tree, a pea seed into a pea plant and so on.
Extension: Investigate flower structure. Discuss how flowers are pollinated before seed development begins.

Page 7: Food from plants

Key idea: We can eat parts of some plants.
Developing the investigation: Discuss the names of the various parts of a plant (see the worksheet on page 31).
Likely outcome: Parts of the plant eaten are: leaves - cabbage and lettuce; root - carrots and beetroot; fruit - apple, plum and grapes; seeds - peas and peanuts.
Extension: Discuss what parts of plants the children have already eaten today.

Page 8: Fruit and vegetables

Key ideas: We eat both fruit and vegetables. The differences between fruit and vegetables.
Developing the investigation: Remind the children that a fruit contains seeds; a vegetable is a leaf, stem, root, shoot, bud or even a flower.
Likely outcomes: Fruit: apple, orange, runner bean, pear and strawberry; vegetables: carrot, potato, cabbage and onion.
   Carrots, potatoes and onions grow in the ground. Apples, pears and oranges grow on trees, while runner beans, cabbages and strawberries grow on smaller plants.
Extension: Discuss the forms in which our fruit and vegetables come, such as fresh and frozen.

Page 9: Fruit colours

Key idea: Many fruit are brightly coloured.
Extension: Discuss why many fruit are brightly coloured - to attract animals (including humans) that will disperse or scatter the seeds.

Page 10: Packets of seeds

Key ideas: Seeds are sold in packets. Flower seeds grow into flowering plants and vegetable seeds into vegetables.
Extension: Plant some easily grown seeds such as radish, nasturtiums and marigolds.

Page 11: Sorting seeds

Key idea: seeds can be sorted on the basis of colour, shape, size and feel or texture, as well as what kinds of plants they grow into.
Extension: Investigate whether small seeds grow into small plants and large seeds into large plants. Discuss how to measure the size of seeds.

Page 12: Measure some seeds

Key ideas: Seeds differ greatly in size. It is possible to measure small objects such as seeds.
Developing the investigation: Discuss the children's ideas on how to measure small objects.

Page 13: Runner bean seeds

Key idea: Runner bean seeds show considerable variation in colour and patterning.
Extension: Discuss the ways in which other living things, including humans, vary.

Page 14: Inside a broad bean seed

Key ideas: All seeds consist of a seed coat enclosing a food store and an embryo plant.
Developing the investigation: Discuss why the embryo plant needs a food store.
Extension: Examine other large seeds, such as acorns and conkers. Will half a seed grow?

Page 15: Warmth and cold

Key idea: Seeds require warm conditions if they are to germinate.
Developing the investigation: Discuss the difference between the conditions on a sunny window-sill and in the refrigerator.
Likely outcome: As long as the paper towelling is kept moist, the seeds on the warm window-sill will

germinate quickly whereas those in the refrigerator will germinate very slowly, if at all.
Extension: Discuss the effects of warmth and cold on other living things, including humans.

Page 16: Hairy clowns

Key ideas: Seeds need warmth and moisture to grow. To produce healthy seedlings, seeds also need light.
Likely outcome: The seeds without moisture will not grow. The seeds on the sunny window-sill will produce short, dark-green shoots ('hair'), while the seeds placed in the dark cupboard will produce yellow, straggly seedlings.
Extension: See the effect lack of light has on grass plants by covering part of a lawn for a few days.

Page 17: Which way up?

Key idea: Even if seeds are planted upside-down, the roots always grow down and the shoots always grow up to the light.
Developing the investigation: Before the seeds are turned into a new position, ask the children what they think will happen.
Likely outcome: The roots of the seedlings will curve round to grow downwards and the shoots will grow upwards.

Page 18: Watch your seeds grow

Key idea: The root emerges from a seed first, to be followed later by the shoot.
Extension: Find ways of measuring the growth of the root and shoot of each seedling.

Page 19: Measure a runner bean

Key ideas: Seedlings grow in height. A runner bean plant produces flowers and then seeds.
Extension: Measure the growth of some quick-growing seedlings such as cress, grass or maize.

Page 20: Make a runner bean maze

Key idea: A runner bean will bend from side to side as it grows in order to reach the light.
Developing the investigation: Ask the children to predict what will happen.
Likely outcome: The bean shoot will bend as it grows and ultimately emerge from the hole in the box to reach the light.

Page 21: Growing acorns

Key ideas: A tree is a large plant which bears seeds. Acorns can be grown, just like other seeds.
Developing the investigation: Discuss whether trees have flowers. Although some trees, such as the apple, pear and plum, have bright, conspicuous flowers, others, such as oak, ash and beech are dull, green and inconspicuous.
Likely outcome: The best time to do this activity is autumn or early winter. At that time the acorns will grow quite quickly, whereas at other times, germination may take many months.
Extension: Grow other tree seeds, pips, stones and nuts. In the spring, plant out the seedlings of native trees in a garden.

Page 22: Grow some pips and stones

Key idea: The pips and stones from the fruit we eat will grow into seedling trees.
Developing the investigation: Discuss the climates of the countries where the fruit we eat grows.
Likely outcome: Most pips and stones from ripe fruit will germinate and produce seedling trees.
Extension: Plant peanuts (unroasted and unsalted) in pots of soil on the window-sill.

Page 23: Scattering seeds

Key idea: Fruit and seeds have to be dispersed or scattered to prevent overcrowding in the vicinity of the parent plant.
Developing the investigation: Discuss why fruit and seeds are often produced in great number and why they have to be scattered from the parent plant.
Likely outcome: Wind dispersed: dandelion. Cling to the fur of animals: goosegrass and burdock. Eaten by birds and other animals and the seeds dropped: hawthorn fruits and elderberries.

Page 24: Dandelion clock

Key idea: The seeds of the dandelion each have a 'parachute' which carries them in the wind.
Likely outcome: In dry weather, dandelion seeds are dispersed considerable distances by the wind. If the 'parachute' is moistened, the fruit becomes heavier and no longer floats in the air. Therefore, the ideal weather for a dandelion to disperse its seeds would be dry, windy weather. It is not possible to tell the time by a dandelion 'clock'.
Extension: Investigate the dispersal of other seeds with hairs or 'parachutes', such as thistles.

Page 25: Winged fruit

Key idea: If stored in a dry place, the winged fruits of sycamore, maple and ash trees can be kept for many months until they are needed.
Likely outcome: The fruit will twirl to the ground 'like miniature helicopters'. If the wings are removed, the seeds drop straight to the ground.
Extension: Make paper 'spinners' to investigate how tree fruit are able to twirl along in the wind.

Page 26: Seeds we eat

Key ideas: Seeds form an important part of our diet. We eat some seeds direct and others which have been processed into new forms.
Developing the investigation: Discuss how bread is made from wheat seeds.

Likely outcome: Other foods made from seeds include all breakfast cereals, biscuits, pies, puddings, cakes, coffee, nuts, cornflour, semolina, noodles, custard, mustard and pepper.
Extension: Grind wheat and make flour. Make unleavened bread from a sample of this flour.

Page 27: Which seeds do birds like best?

Key ideas: Some wild birds specialise in eating seeds. Not all kinds of seeds are equally palatable to birds.
Developing the investigation: Explain that birds with short, stout beaks, such as sparrows, finches and buntings, specialise in eating seeds.
Likely outcome: It is not possible to predict the outcome of this experiment, but usually cereal grains come high in the list of preferred seeds.

Page 28: Garden weeds

Key ideas: Weeds are plants growing in places where they are not wanted. Weeds have a very short life cycle.
Developing the investigation: Discuss what is meant by a 'weed.
Likely outcome: The weed plant will be found to have a very short life cycle, often just a few weeks from seed back to seed stage again.

Page 29: Grow cuttings

Key idea: Cuttings are one way of growing a new plant without seeds.

Likely outcome: Most of the suggested cuttings grow roots within a few weeks. They can then be transferred to pots of moist soil or compost.
Extension: Investigate how strawberry plants spread. As well as spreading by seeds, they produce stems, or runners, that radiate out from the parent plant and, on the ends of these, new plants grow.

Page 30: Growing bulbs

Key ideas: Bulbs are modified budsand are another way of producing new plants without the need for seeds.
Developing the investigation: Discuss the various kinds of bulbs that the children are familiar with. Carefully cut an onion bulb in half and examine the small bud in the centre which is surrounded by modified leaves swollen with food.
Likely outcome: The onion bulb will soon produce roots and shoots. It will grow even if not placed first in the dark, but will take much longer.

Page 31: The parts of a plant

Key idea: A revision item to help children to remember the names of the parts of a plant.

Page 32: Beans and light

Key idea: Plants grow towards the light.
Likely outcome: As it grows, the bean plant will bend over towards the light coming through the hole in the box.

National Curriculum: Science

In addition to the PoS for AT1, the following PoS are relevant to this book:

AT2 - Pupils should:
• be introduced to the main parts of flowering plants and investigate what plants need to grow and reproduce.
• have opportunities, when possible through first-hand observation, to find out about a variety of animal and plant life and become aware, that some life-forms became extinct a long time ago and others more recently. They should sort living things into broad groups according to similarities and differences using observable features. Over a period of time, pupils should take responsibility for the care of living things, maintaining their welfare by knowing about their needs and understanding the care required.
• Study plants and animals in a variety of local habitats, for example, *playing field, garden* and *pond*. They should discuss how human activity produces local changes in the environment.
• Drawing upon their study of living things in school and the local environment, they should be introduced to the idea that plants are the ultimate source of all food in the living world.

AT4 - Pupils should:
• observe closely the natural environment to detect seasonal changes, including length of daylight, weather and changes in plants and animals and relate these to the passage of time.

Scottish 5 - 14 Curriculum

Environmental studies
Attainment outcomes: Science in the environment (living things; processes of life; conservation and care of living things)
                       Investigating (finding out; recording; interpreting; reporting)

▲ Name _____

Fruit and seeds

You will need: a pencil.

Seeds grow inside fruit.

Seeds are smaller than the fruit they grow in.

▲ Look at these pictures.

▲ Label the fruit.

▲ Label the seeds.

▲ Draw some more fruit and seeds.

▲ ESSENTIALS FOR SCIENCE: Seeds and seedlings

▲ Name _____

From plant to seed

You will need: a pencil.

All plants have flowers.

The flowers turn into fruit with seeds inside.

▲ Use the chart to label the pictures. Find more plants, fruit and seeds to enter in the chart.

Plant	Fruit	Seed
Oak tree	Acorn + cup	Acorn
Pea plant	Pea pod	Pea seed

▲ ESSENTIALS FOR SCIENCE: Seeds and seedlings

▲ Name _____

Food from plants

You will need: a pencil.

We can eat the parts of some plants.

▲ Tick the right box for the part we eat.

	Leaves	Roots	Fruit	Seeds
Carrots				
Apples				
Lettuce				
Plums				
Beetroot				
Cabbage				
Peas				
Grapes				
Peanuts				

▲ ESSENTIALS FOR SCIENCE: Seeds and seedlings

▲ Name _____

Fruit and vegetables

You will need: a pencil.

▲ Which is a fruit? Write **f** in the box.

▲ Find out where each of these grows. Do they grow in the ground, on a tree, or on a smaller plant?

▲ ESSENTIALS FOR SCIENCE: Seeds and seedlings

▲ Name _____

Fruit colours

You will need: coloured pencils, paints or crayons.

▲ Look at the picture below.

▲ Colour it in.

▲ Draw and colour some more fruit.

▲ ESSENTIALS FOR SCIENCE: Seeds and seedlings

▲ Name _____

Packets of seeds

You will need: a pencil; a ruler.

Many shops sell seeds.

Some of the seeds are vegetable seeds.

Some of the seeds are flower seeds.

▲ Look at the seed packets below. What do you think the seeds in them will grow into?

▲ Join each packet with the name of the plant which the seeds will grow into.

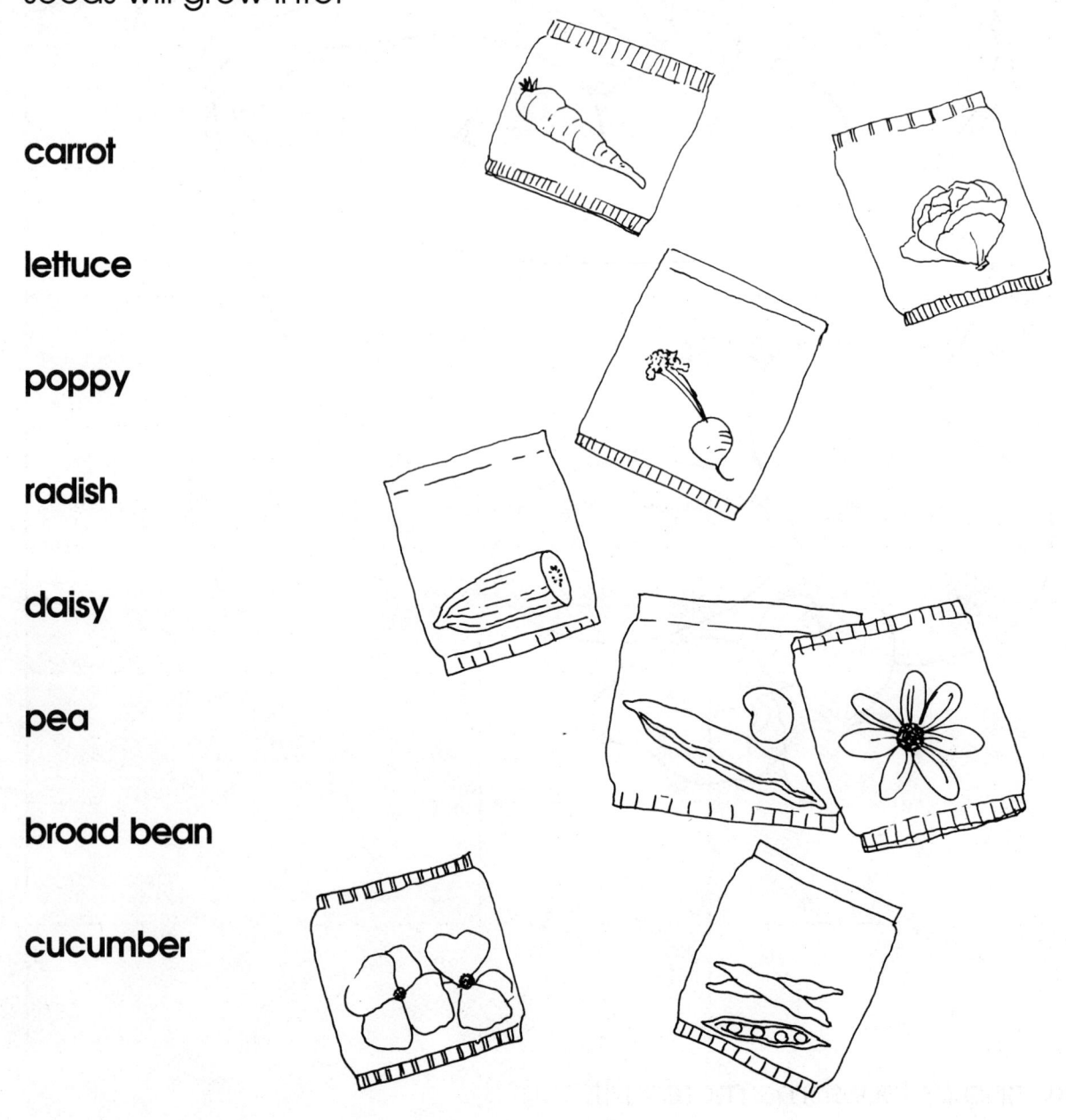

carrot

lettuce

poppy

radish

daisy

pea

broad bean

cucumber

▲ ESSENTIALS FOR SCIENCE: Seeds and seedlings   10

▲ Name _____

Sorting seeds

You will need: seeds of as many kinds as possible, including rice, maize, oats, nuts, beans, peas, wild-bird food, pet food.

▲ Find as many seeds as you can.

▲ How many different ways can you sort them?

   Colour?   Shape?   Size?   Feel?

▲ Complete and fill in the chart below.

Seed	Colour			
Pea	Green			
Conker				

▲ Make a picture with some of your seeds.

▲ ESSENTIALS FOR SCIENCE: Seeds and seedlings

▲ Name _____

Measure some seeds

You will need: two blocks of wood; a ruler; a pencil; some seeds.

▲ Measure some seeds.

▲ Put a seed between two blocks of wood.

▲ Measure the gap between the blocks of wood.

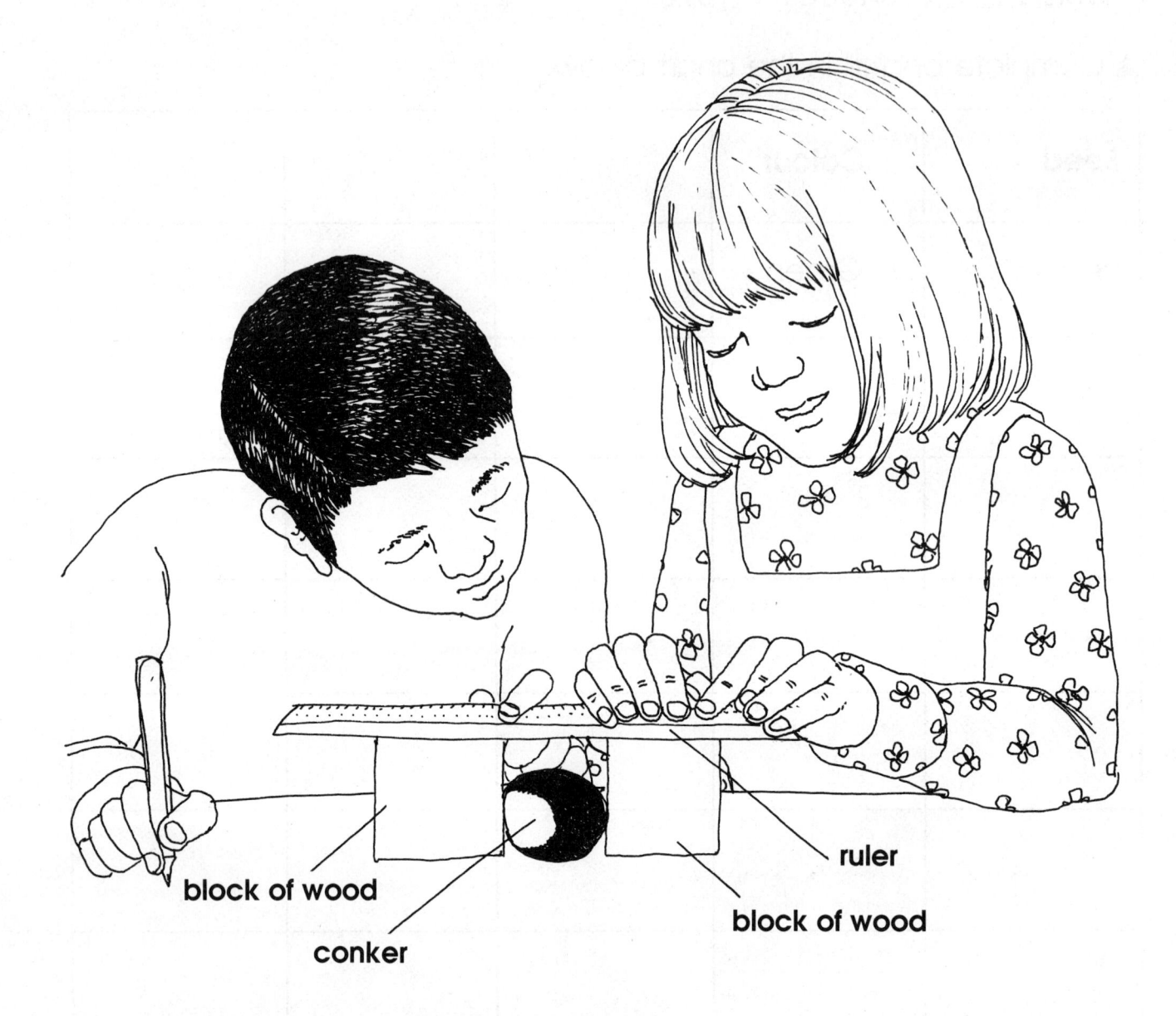

block of wood

conker

ruler

block of wood

▲ What is the largest seed you can find?

▲ Which is the smallest?

▲ Can you weigh seeds? Try it.

▲ ESSENTIALS FOR SCIENCE: Seeds and seedlings

▲ Name _____

Runner bean seeds

You will need: runner bean seeds; hand lens; a pencil; coloured pencils or crayons.

▲ Look at the runner bean seeds carefully.

What colours are they?

What patterns do they have on them?

Can you find two runner beans exactly alike?

▲ Draw some of your runner beans.

▲ Colour them.

▲ ESSENTIALS FOR SCIENCE: Seeds and seedlings

▲ Name _____

Inside a broad bean seed

You will need: a dish of cold water; a broad bean seed; a hand lens; a pencil.

▲ Soak a broad bean seed in cold water overnight.

▲ The next day, carefully split the seed open.

▲ Look at the inside of the bean with a hand lens.

Can you see a tiny plant? It is called an embryo.

Can you see a food store? The tiny plant uses this food when it grows.

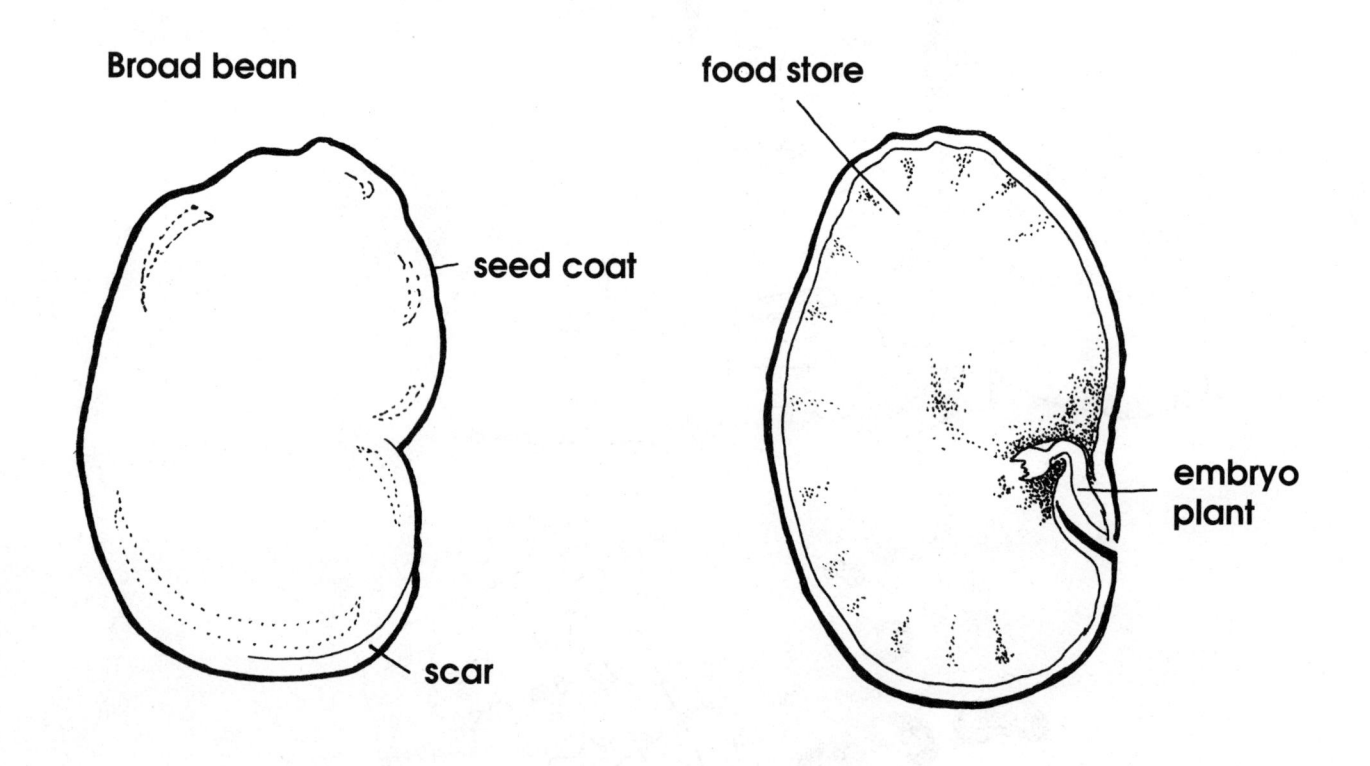

Broad bean

— seed coat

— scar

food store —

embryo plant —

▲ Now look at the insides of other seeds.

Do they all have an embryo?

Do they all have a food store?

▲ ESSENTIALS FOR SCIENCE: Seeds and seedlings

▲ Name _____

Warmth and cold

You will need: cress seeds; paper towels; two saucers.

▲ Wet the paper towels. Line the saucers with them.

▲ Sprinkle cress seeds on both saucers.

▲ Put one saucer in a warm place. Put the other saucer in a refrigerator.

▲ Look at the seeds each day.

▲ Do not let the paper towels dry out.

▲ What happens? Do cress seeds grow best in a warm place or a cold place?

▲ Try growing some other seeds in the same way.

▲ ESSENTIALS FOR SCIENCE: Seeds and seedlings

▲ Name _____

Hairy clowns

You will need: three clean yoghurt pots; cotton wool or paper towels; cress seeds or grass seeds; felt-tipped pens; a pencil.

▲ Draw a face on each pot.

▲ Fill the pots with cotton wool or paper towels.

▲ Wet the cotton wool or paper towels in two of the pots.

▲ Sprinkle seeds on all three pots.

▲ Put one of the pots with wet cotton wool or towels in a dark cupboard.

▲ Put the other two pots on a sunny window-sill.

▲ Do all three clowns grow hair?

▲ Do all three lots of seeds grow the same?

▲ ESSENTIALS FOR SCIENCE: Seeds and seedlings

▲ Name _____

Which way up?

You will need: a block of wood; paper towels; pea seeds; a strip of clear plastic; three drawing-pins; a shallow dish of water; a pencil.

▲ Put paper towels around the wood.

▲ Lay two pea seeds on the paper towels.

▲ Wrap the plastic round the seeds and the wood. Fix it with the drawing-pins.

▲ Stand the block in a dish of water.

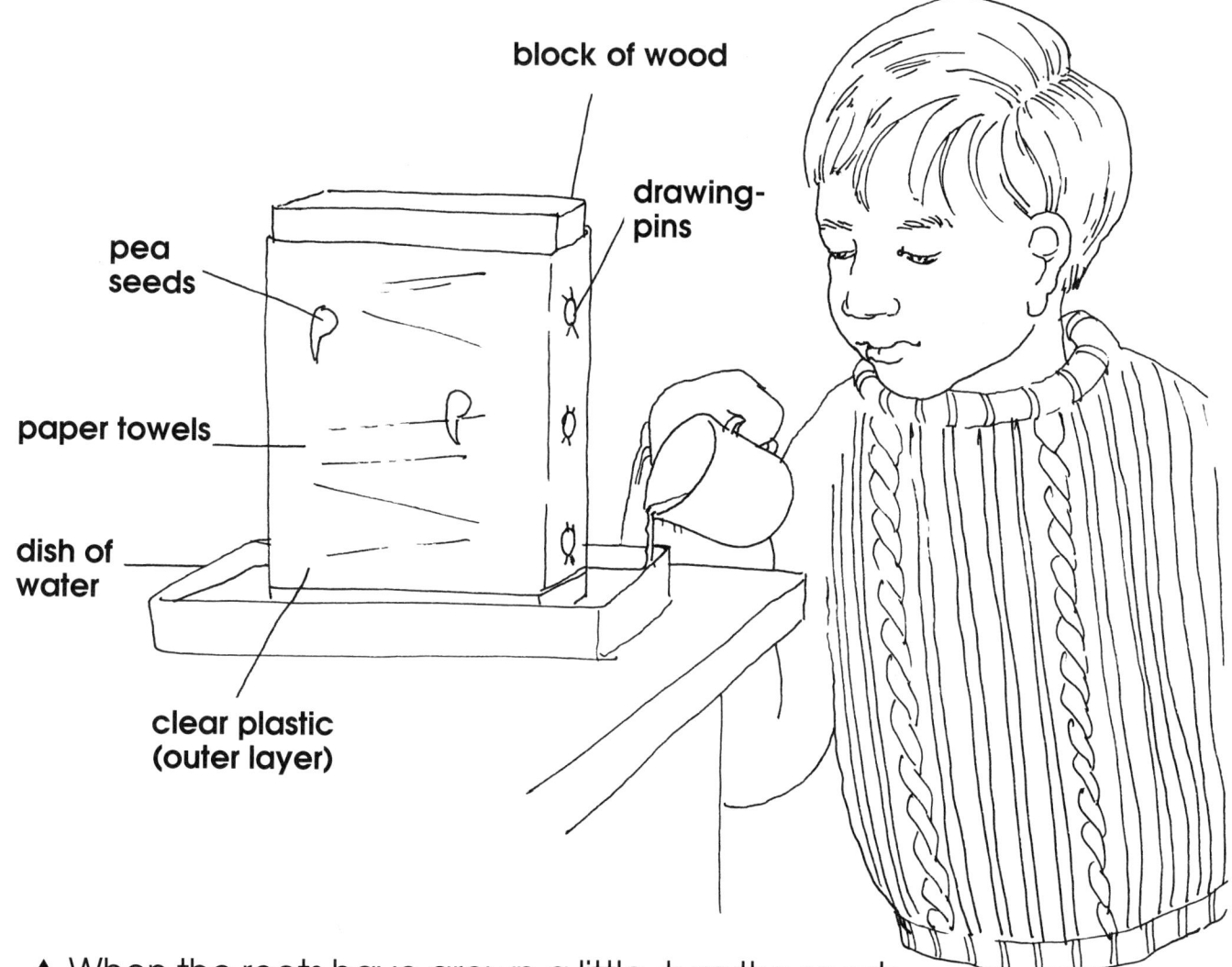

Labels: block of wood; drawing-pins; pea seeds; paper towels; dish of water; clear plastic (outer layer)

▲ When the roots have grown a little, turn the seeds the other way up.

What happens to the roots?

What happens if you plant seeds upside down?

▲ ESSENTIALS FOR SCIENCE: Seeds and seedlings

▲ Name _____

Watch your seeds grow

You will need: pea, bean or radish seeds; a hand lens; a see-through plastic beaker; paper towels; a pencil.

▲ Line the inside of the beaker with paper towels.

▲ Put about 2cm of water in the beaker.

▲ Put some seeds between the paper towels and the beaker.

paper towels

water level

▲ Watch carefully what happens to the seeds.

▲ After a few days your seeds begin to grow. Use a hand lens to look at your seedlings.

▲ Draw your seedlings.

▲ Do all seeds grow in the same way?

▲ ESSENTIALS FOR SCIENCE: Seeds and seedlings

▲ Name _____

Measure a runner bean

You will need: a runner bean seed; a flower pot; soil; a stick; a pencil.

▲ Plant a runner bean seed in a pot of soil.

▲ Measure your bean seed when it starts to grow.

▲ Measure your bean plant each week.

▲ Write down how much your bean plant grows each week.

▲ When the plant has grown tall, give it a stick to climb.

▲ Does your bean plant grow flowers? Does it grow beans?

▲ Grow a pea seed in the same way.

▲ ESSENTIALS FOR SCIENCE: Seeds and seedlings

▲ Name _____

Make a runner bean maze

You will need: a runner bean seedling; a shoe box with a lid; scissors; cardboard; sticky tape; a pencil.

▲ Cut a small hole in one end of the box.

▲ Fix three pieces of cardboard in the box as shown below.

▲ Stand the bean plant at one end of the box. Put the lid on the box.

▲ Stand the box on a window-sill. Leave it for a few days.

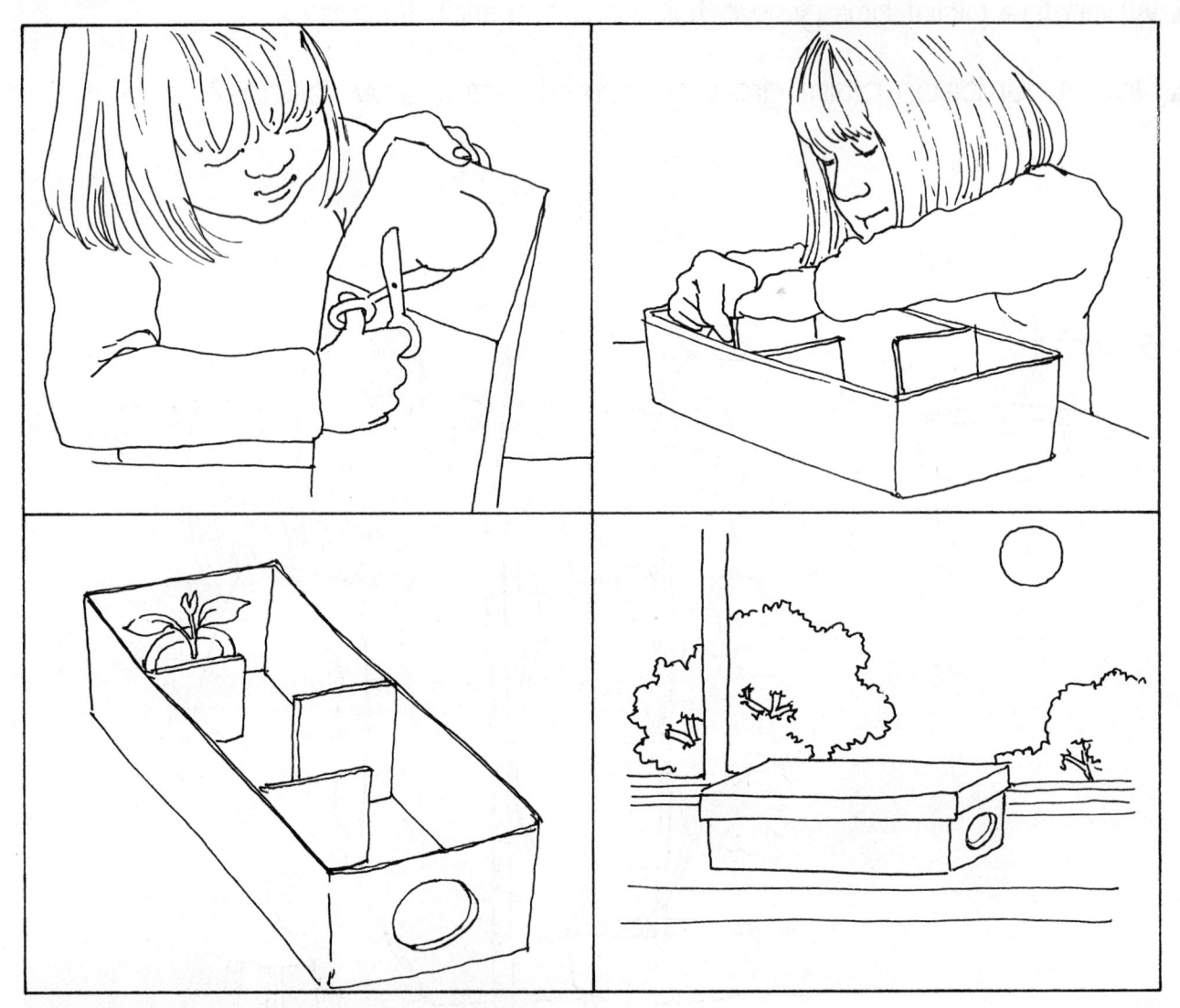

▲ Lift the lid of the box carefully.

▲ What has happened to the bean plant? Why is this?

▲ Will a pea seedling do the same thing?

▲ ESSENTIALS FOR SCIENCE: Seeds and seedlings

▲ Name _____

Growing acorns

You will need: acorns; a flower pot; some soil; a bottle of water; a pencil.

A tree is a very big plant.

Trees have seeds. The acorn is the seed of an oak tree.

▲ Grow some acorn seeds. You can grow them in soil. Make sure that the pointed end of the acorn is at the top.

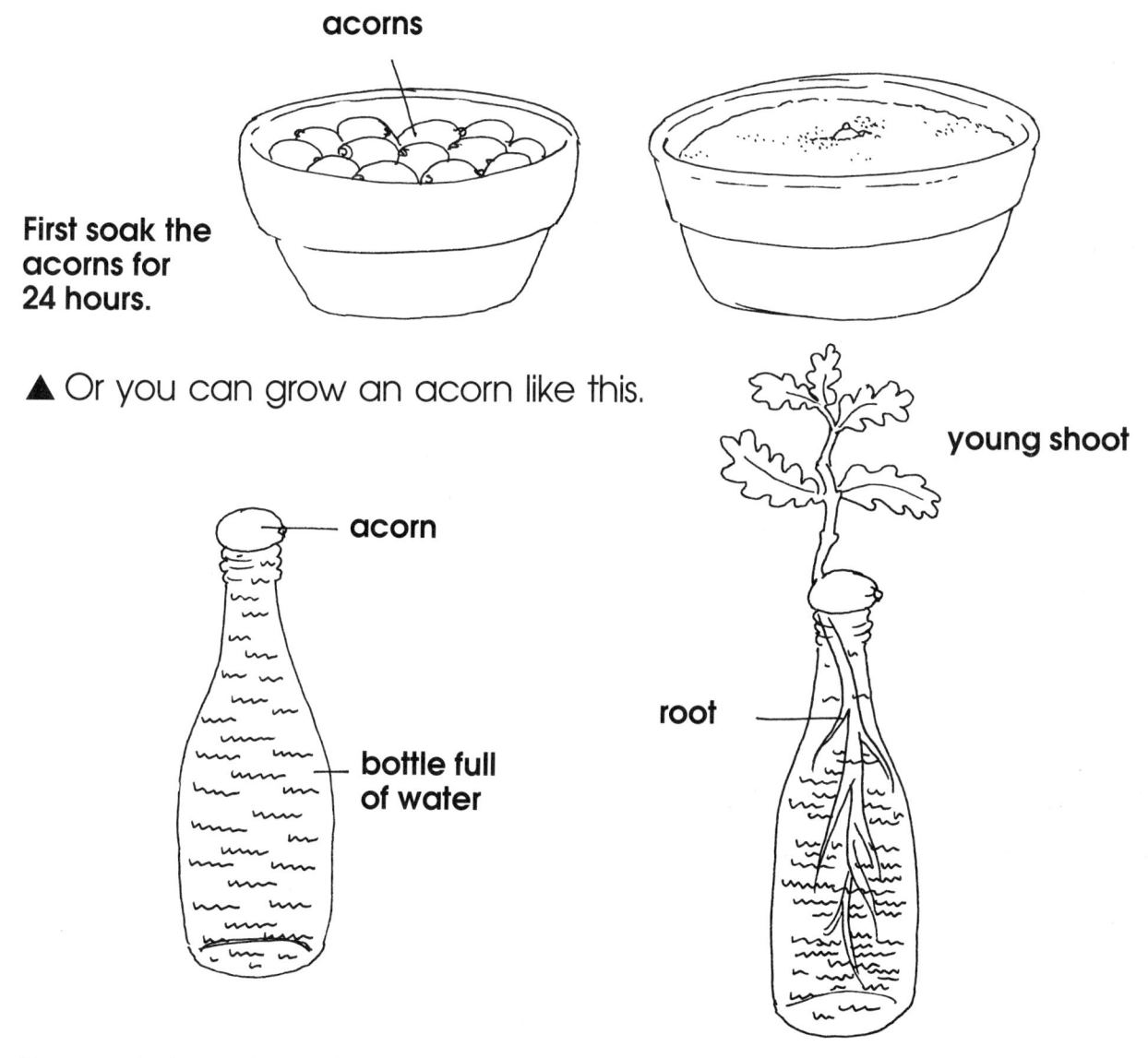

acorns

First soak the acorns for 24 hours.

▲ Or you can grow an acorn like this.

acorn

bottle full of water

young shoot

root

It may take a long time for your acorns to grow.

▲ Draw pictures of them as they grow.

▲ Try growing conkers and other tree seeds in this way.

▲ ESSENTIALS FOR SCIENCE: Seeds and seedlings

▲ Name _____

Grow some pips and stones

You will need: orange, grapefruit, apple and pear pips; plum stones; small flower pots; soil; small plastic bags; elastic bands.

Pips and stones are seeds with hard coats.

▲ Grow some seeds in pots.

▲ Water the soil.

▲ Push two or three seeds in a little way into the soil.

▲ Cover each pot with a plastic bag and fix it with an elastic band.

▲ Stand your pots on a sunny window-sill. Keep them covered until the pips start to grow.

▲ Try to grow other pips and stones in this way.

▲ ESSENTIALS FOR SCIENCE: Seeds and seedlings

▲ Name _____

Scattering seeds

You will need: a pencil; a ruler.

Some fruit and seeds blow in the wind.

Some fruit and seeds stick to animals' fur.

Some fruit are eaten by animals and they drop the seeds.

▲ Look at these pictures. Draw a line from the fruit or seed to the picture of how you think it might be scattered.

▲ ESSENTIALS FOR SCIENCE: Seeds and seedlings   23

▲ Name _____

Dandelion clock

You will need: some dandelion 'clocks'; a very long tape measure.

▲ Count how many seeds there are in a dandelion clock.

▲ Blow another dandelion clock.

How many blows do you take to blow away all the seeds?

How many metres do the seeds travel?

Can you really tell the time with a dandelion clock?

▲ Moisten the parachute of a dandelion seed. Does it float in the air now?

▲ What kind of weather would be best for a dandelion to scatter its seeds?

▲ ESSENTIALS FOR SCIENCE: Seeds and seedlings

▲ Name _____

Winged fruit

You will need: winged fruit from the sycamore, maple and ash trees; scissors; a pencil.

Some tree fruit have wings.

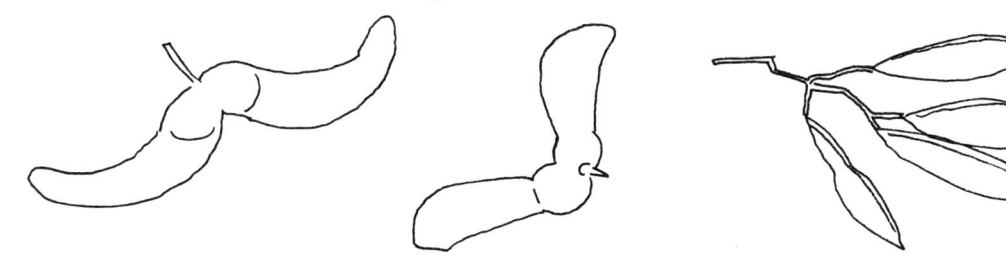

▲ Drop one of the fruit from a high place. Watch it fall.

▲ What does it do?

▲ Cut off the wings.

▲ Drop the fruit again. Does it fall in the same way as before?

▲ Now try this with the other winged fruit.

▲ ESSENTIALS FOR SCIENCE: Seeds and seedlings

▲ Name _____

Seeds we eat

You will need: a pencil.

We eat lots of different seeds.

We also eat food made from seeds.

▲ Write in the boxes what the food is.

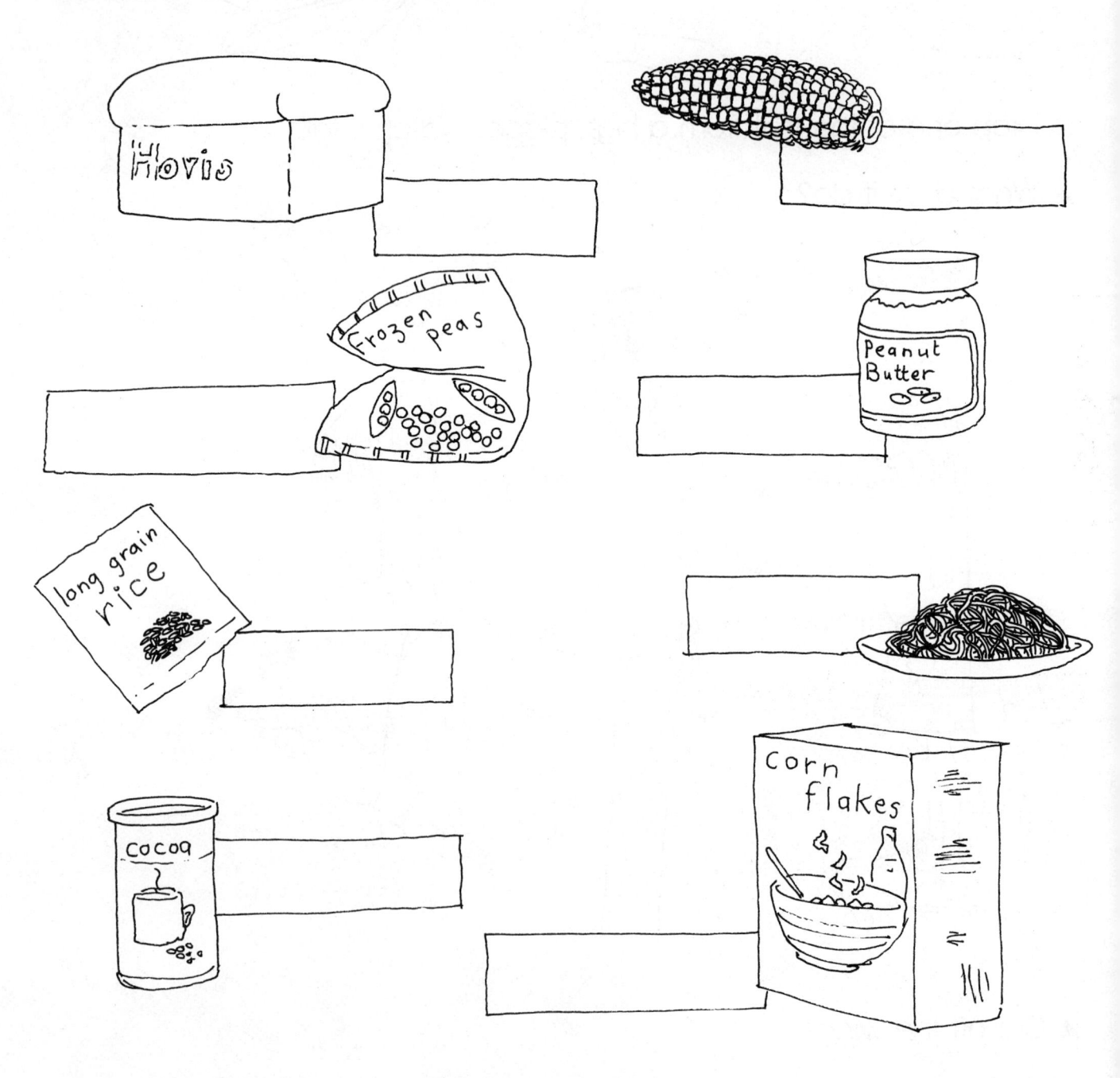

▲ Is the food a seed or made from seeds?

▲ How many more foods made from seeds can you find?

▲ ESSENTIALS FOR SCIENCE: Seeds and seedlings

▲ Name _____

Which seeds do birds like best?

You will need: small lids; a plank of wood; a hammer; small nails; seeds of different kinds; a pencil.

▲ Ask an adult to help you nail the lids on to a plank.

▲ Put different seeds in each lid.

▲ Put the plank on a lawn where the birds can see it.

▲ Watch carefully.

Which seeds do the birds like best?

▲ Try the birds with some fruit.

Which fruit do they like best?

▲ Record your results below.

▲ ESSENTIALS FOR SCIENCE: Seeds and seedlings

▲ Name _____

Garden weeds

You will need: plant pots; soil or compost; seeds of a garden weed such as groundsel, chick weed, dandelion or shepherd's purse; a pencil.

Weed seeds grow quickly.

▲ Plant some weed seeds in a pot.

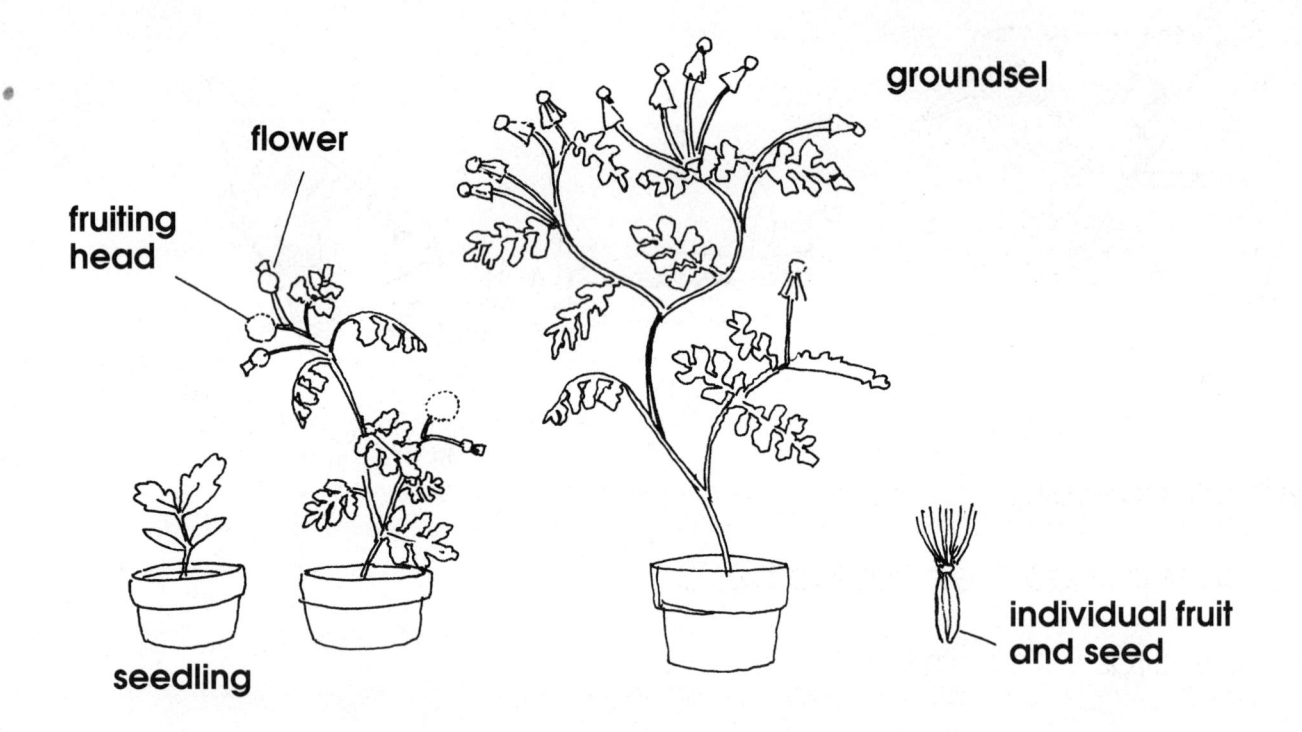

fruiting head

flower

groundsel

seedling

individual fruit and seed

▲ When do the seeds start to grow?

▲ When does the plant have its first leaves?

▲ How long does it take for flowers to form?

▲ When does the plant make seeds?

▲ Grow some of these seeds.

▲ Draw each of the stages in the life of your weed.

▲ ESSENTIALS FOR SCIENCE: Seeds and seedlings

▲ Name _____

Grow cuttings

You will need: a plastic bottle; a piece of busy lizzie, mint, willow or geranium.

You do not always need seeds to grow new plants.

You can grow new plants from pieces of plant.

▲ Take off some of the bottom leaves of a plant, as shown below.

▲ Put the piece of plant in the bottle.

▲ Put the water in the bottle.

busy lizzie plant

Cut the shoot below a leaf, leaving a short length of stem.

Trim the end.

Gently remove the lower leaves.

Stand the shoot in a small bottle of water.

▲ Stand your bottle on a window-sill.

One day roots may start to grow from your plant. It may take a long time.

▲ Try to grow cuttings of other plants like this.

▲ ESSENTIALS FOR SCIENCE: Seeds and seedlings

▲ Name _____

Growing bulbs

You will need: a plastic jar; a yoghurt pot; an onion; scissors; water.

An onion is a kind of bulb.

▲ Grow an onion.

▲ Ask an adult to cut the bottom from the yoghurt pot.

▲ Push the pot into the jar. Fill the jar with water.

▲ Stand the onion in the pot.

▲ Put the onion in a dark cupboard for a week or two.

▲ Then put it on a sunny window-sill.

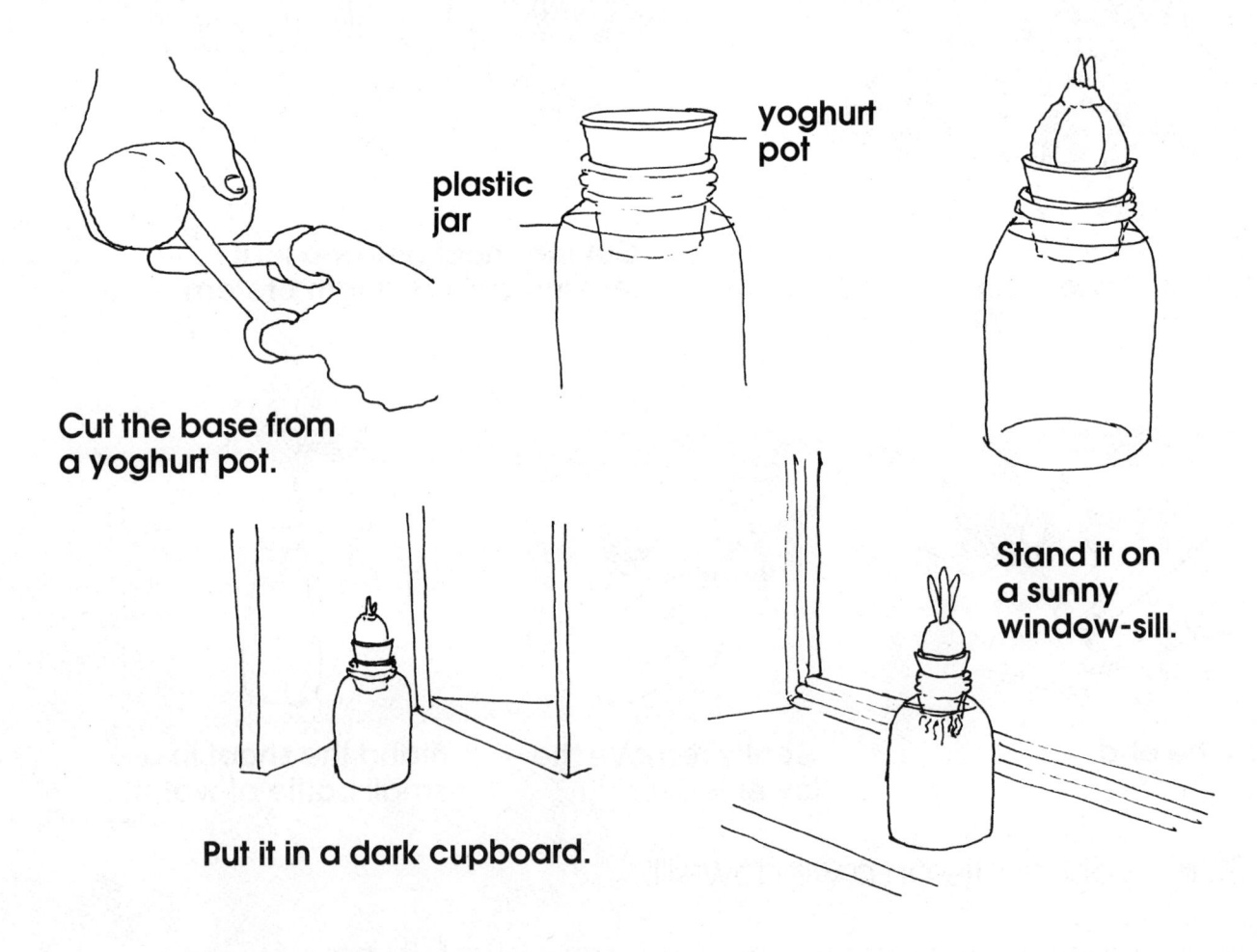

Cut the base from a yoghurt pot.

plastic jar

yoghurt pot

Put it in a dark cupboard.

Stand it on a sunny window-sill.

▲ Watch the new onion plant grow.

▲ Try to grow other bulbs like this.

▲ ESSENTIALS FOR SCIENCE: Seeds and seedlings

▲ Name _____

The parts of a plant

You will need: a pencil; a ruler.

▲ Look at the picture.

▲ Join the names to the right parts of the plant.

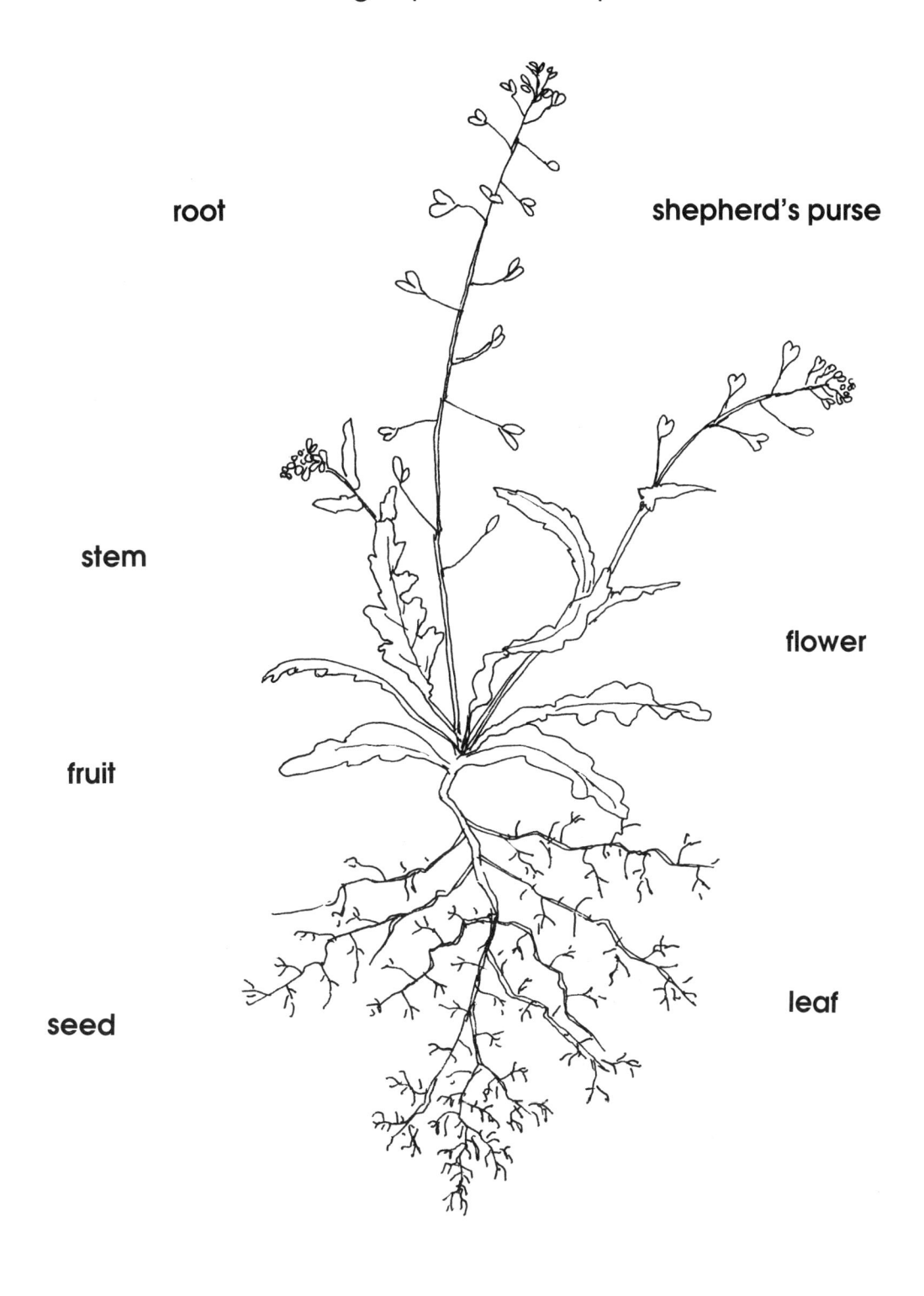

root

shepherd's purse

stem

flower

fruit

seed

leaf

▲ ESSENTIALS FOR SCIENCE: Seeds and seedlings

▲ Name _____

Beans and light

You will need: a cardboard box; a plant pot; a runner bean seed; soil or compost.

▲ Plant the bean seed in a plant pot of soil or compost.

▲ Keep the bean seed well watered.

▲ Wait until the bean seedling is about 15cm high.

▲ Cut a hole in the box.

▲ Put the box over the seedling. Make sure that the hole faces a window.

▲ After two or three days lift the box.

▲ What has happened to the bean?

▲ Can you make the bean grow round in a circle?

▲ ESSENTIALS FOR SCIENCE: Seeds and seedlings

Contents

Teachers' notes	1
Living and non-living	5
A rainbow girl	6
A body game	7
Body measurements	8
What I can do with my body	9
Your weight	10
Your face	11
Make face masks	12
Hair	13
Your teeth	14
Senses	15
Tongues	16
Eyes	17
Can we believe our eyes?	18
Food	19
Food from animals and plants	20
The skeleton	21
Joints	22
Listen to your heartbeat	23
Breathing	24
Growing	25
You as a baby	26
Me and my friends	27
How good is your memory?	28
Which side of your body do you use the most?	29
Handprints	30
Measuring hands	31
All about me	32

Teachers' notes

Aims of this book

The aims of this book are:
- to show that all humans are built on the same basic pattern;
- to introduce the names of the main parts of the body and their functions;
- to show that humans vary and that we are all individuals;
- to provide a means of introducing basic ideas on health education;
- to form the foundation for simple ideas on genetics and evolution;
- to help children to understand that individual differences in rates of growth and development are quite normal.

Developing science skills

While it is not essential to follow the order of the worksheets, it is important that all those covering one aspect of a subject, such as the senses, are dealt with at approximately the same time.

It is important to remember that, although it is in the *doing* of science that children learn best, this involves more than just practical work. They need to observe, record, predict, measure, look for patterns, classify, explain and ask questions that can lead to further investigations. They need time to discuss their work, before and after the activity; this will also aid the teacher in monitoring the children's progress so that they build a valid framework for future development.

Safety precautions

The activities described on the worksheets mainly use everyday items of equipment and materials which are perfectly safe if used sensibly. Where extra care is necessary on safety grounds, this is mentioned both on the worksheets and also in the appropriate section of the teachers' notes.

There are two general safety precautions to take when teaching children about the workings of the human body. When discussing human variation, a particularly sensitive approach is needed when considering, for example, whether tall children have tall parents or whether blue-eyed parents have blue-eyed children. It is essential that children who are adopted, fostered, 'in care', or members of one-parent families, should not be made to feel unfortunate, abnormal, unusual or in any way different. It is also important that young children do not learn to associate any partss of their bodies with adult disapproval.

Scientific background

This information seeks to help you to understand the scientific concepts and ideas covered in this book. It generally goes beyond the level of understanding expected of most children, but will give you the confidence to ask and answer questions and to guide the children in their investigations.

The human species

People of all races, classes, colour or nationality belong to a single species, *Homo sapiens*. They share unique characteristics, such as a high degree of intelligence associated with a large, rounded skull, upright posture and the ability to communicate verbally.

▲ ESSENTIALS FOR SCIENCE: Ourselves

Variation

Although no two people are alike (not even identical twins), all people have the same general body shape and the same internal structure. There are two broad types of variation. It is possible to arrange even a relatively small group of people into a continuous line – lightest to heaviest or tallest to shortest. Characteristics like these, in which there are many intermediates between the two extremes, are said to show continuous variation. Intelligence and human skin colour show continuous variation. The latter is due to a brown pigment, melanin, which protects the body from the harmful effects of the sun's rays. The different amounts of melanin in the skin cause the shade of colour of the various races.

Other characteristics have no, or very few, intermediate forms. People are, with rare exceptions, either male or female. They can or cannot roll their tongues into a U-shape. Everyone belongs to one of the four main blood groups.

Inheritance

An individual inherits characteristics from both parents, although what they are is due to chance. For example, she may inherit hair and eye colour from one or both parents, together with features such as the shape of the nose, ears and mouth. These hereditary characteristics are fixed from the moment or conception.

Environmental influences

Some of the traits we inherit can be altered by environmental influences, such as diet, activity, education, health and even wealth. Continuous variations are the ones most likely to be affected by the environment. The limit to a person's height, for example, is inherited, yet whether we achieve that potential maximum height depends on the nature of our diet, health and levels of exercise during the formative years.

Notes on individual activities

Page 5: Living and non-living

Key idea: there are differences between living and non-living things.
Likely outcome: living things: plant, earthworm, frog, child, tree, butterfly, dog. Non-living things: comb, television set, cup and saucer, motorcycle, teddy bear.
Developing the investigation: discuss living things – they feed, move, grow, breathe, excrete, reproduce and respond to changes. Do vehicles move because they are alive? Is a house under construction alive because it grows?

Page 6: A rainbow girl

Key idea: the parts of the body have their own individual names.
Developing the investigation: discuss the functions of the various parts of the body.

Page 7: A body game

Key idea: the parts of the body have their own names.
Extension activity: repeat this activity, naming parts of the head and face or parts of the limbs.

Page 8: Body measurements

Key idea: there are large variations among people in the measurements of parts of the body, even among children of similar age.
Developing the investigation: measure the variation in other parts of the body, such as head circumference and middle finger length.

Page 9: What I can do with my body

Key idea: we use different parts of the body for different activities.
Likely outcome: reading – hands and eyes; writing – hands and eyes; swimming, running, cycling and dancing – the whole body; watching television – the eyes and ears; listening to the radio – the ears.
Developing the investigation: discuss the value of physical exercise in strengthening the body.

Page 10: Your weight

Specialist equipment: bathroom scales.
Key idea: there is considerable variation in weight, even amongst children of similar ages.
Developing the investigation: use the bathroom scales to see how hard the children can push with one finger, one hand, both hands, one foot, both feet, and so on.

Page 11: Your face

Key idea: no two faces are exactly alike. Facial expressions are used to show moods or emotions.
Extension activity: ask the children to describe their likes and dislikes.

Page 12: Make face masks

Key idea: facial expressions are used to show moods or emotions.
Likely outcome: the children will probably have difficulty matching the mood of the character in their play to the appropriate facial expression.
Extension activity: devise a mime or a short play. Discuss the role of the eyes in facial expressions.

Page 13: Hair

Key idea: there is individual variation in hair colour, texture, thickness and strength.

▲ ESSENTIALS FOR SCIENCE: Ourselves

Extension activity: do hairs from different people differ in appearance?

Page 14: Your teeth

Key idea: we have different numbers of teeth.
Likely outcome: a complete set of baby or milk teeth is 20. Adults have 32 teeth. The baby teeth normally start to loosen and fall out between the ages of six and twelve years. The biscuit will collect mainly in the crevices between the teeth and in the hollows and grooves at the tops of the back or 'double' teeth.
Extension activity: look at animals' teeth.

Page 15: Senses

Key idea: we have five main senses – sight, hearing, smell, touch and taste.
Likely outcome: you see with your eyes; you hear with your ears; smell with your nose; touch with your hands (or, more accurately, your skin); taste with your tongue. Sight is used the most. When eating food, we use our senses of sight, touch, taste and smell.
Extension activity: discuss how our senses keep us safe.

Page 16: Tongues

Key idea: tongue size and shape varies from individual to individual. Tongue rolling is an inherited characteristic; it cannot be learned unless the ability is already present.
Likely outcome: no amount of practice will turn a non-tongue-roller into someone with that ability.
Developing the investigation: devise ways of showing the vital role of the tongue in speech.
Extension activity: survey how many people have lobed bases to their ears and how many have ears with no distinct lobe (another characteristic).

Page 17: Eyes

Key idea: eye colour varies from individual to individual. It is an inherited characteristic.
Extension activity: examine the pupils of the eyes in bright and dim light.

Page 18: Can we believe our eyes?

Key idea: our eyes can sometimes deceive us.
Extension activity: look at coloured objects, first indoors under fluorescent lights, then outside. Do the colours always appear the same?

Page 19: Food

Key idea: we need a variety of foods if we are to grow, be active and stay healthy.
Developing the investigation: make block graphs or pie charts of favourite foods.
Extension activity: look at proteins, carbohydrates and fats, vitamins and mineral salts.

Page 20: Food from animals and plants

Key idea: some of our foods come from animals, others from plants.
Developing the investigation: discuss the origins of common foods, such as bread, eggs and milk.

Page 21: The skeleton

Key idea: The human body is supported by a skeleton of bones.
Likely outcome: the longest individual bones are the leg bones; the shortest that the children can feel are the individual finger and toe bones, although the three tiny bones inside each ear are even smaller.
Developing the investigation: discuss what our bodies would be like if we did not have bones. Compare with those of animals which lack a skeleton, such as earthworms and jellyfish.

Page 22: Joints

Key idea: joints enable the bones to move.
Developing the investigation: discuss where else joints can be found besides in the human body.
Extension activity: show the children a string puppet.

Page 23: Listen to your heartbeat

Key idea: the heart is a kind of pump which drives blood around the body.
Likely outcome: during and after exercise the heart will beat faster than it did when at rest.
Developing the investigation: discuss what the blood does (carries food, oxygen and heat to all parts of the body, removes waste and helps to fight germs).
Safety precautions: all children doing this activity must be physically fit. No child who is excused games or PE activities on medical grounds should be allowed to be the subject of this activity.

Page 24: Breathing

Key ideas: we breathe air to stay alive. We breathe faster during exercise than when at rest.
Extension activity: discuss air pollution and breathing, and air and burning.
Safety precautions: all children doing this activity must be physically fit. No child who is excused games or PE activities on medical grounds should be allowed to carry out this activity.

Page 25: Growing

Key ideas: growth involves changes to the shape and size of the body. The size and styles of our clothing change as we grow older.
Extension activity: compare the handprints of a child and an adult.

Page 26: You as a baby

Key idea: important physical and mental

▲ ESSENTIALS FOR SCIENCE: Ourselves

changes take place between babyhood and childhood.
Developing the investigation: discuss the prolonged care involved in bringing up a baby.

Page 27: Me and my friends
Key idea: a comparison of individual differences.
Extension activity: discuss all the different people involved in keeping children safe and happy.

Page 28: How good is your memory?
Key idea: some people are better at remembering things than others.
Extension activity: see if older children can remember short sequences of numbers or letters. Can memory be improved with practice?

Page 29: Which side of your body do you use the most?
Key idea: people differ in their preference for their right or left hands and other body parts.
Developing the investigation: encourage the children to write or draw with their 'wrong' hand for a few minutes. Do they find it difficult?
Extension activity: devise some more tests to see which foot people prefer to use.

Page 30: Handprints
Key idea: the size, shape and pattern of handprints varies from person to person.
Extension activity: compare foot sizes.

Page 31: Measuring hands
Key idea: simple methods of measuring the area and carrying capacity of the hands.
Extension activity: discuss the advantages of standard units of measurement.

Page 32: All about me
Key idea: a summary of qualities and differences.
Extension activity: find out some famous people.

National Curriculum: Science

These pages support the following requirements of the National Curriculum for Science.

AT2 – Pupils should:
- find out about themselves and develop their ideas about how they grow, feed, move, use their senses and about the stages of human development.
- consider similarities and differences between themselves and other pupils, and understand that individuals are unique.

AT3 – Pupils should:
- collect and find similarities and differences between a variety of everyday materials.

AT4 – Pupils should:
- have opportunities to explore light sources and the effects related to shadow, reflection and colour.

Scottish 5-14 Curriculum: Environmental studies

Attainment outcome	Strand
Science in the environment	Living things – plants and animals including humans; their distinctive features and characteristics Forces – different types of force involved in moving and stopping Energy – different forms, sources and uses Processes of life – conditions for life and growth; life cycles, key life processes such as breathing and movement
Healthy and safe living	Relationships – relationships and feelings, and their influence on behaviour, responsibility Looking after myself – ways of keeping healthy, growth and change, feelings, choices
Investigating	Finding out – implementing plans, using the senses, instruments, measuring devices, books and documents Recording – recording findings in words, diagrams, sketches, graphs
Designing and making	Making – implementing plans; organising and using equipment, materials and workspace effectively Evaluating – commenting on appearances and effectiveness of creations; making modifications

▲ Name _____

Living and non-living

You will need: a pencil; coloured pencils or crayons.

▲ Look at the pictures. Which of them are of living things?
▲ Colour the living things.

▲ Using the back of this page, make a list of some more living things.

▲ ESSENTIALS FOR SCIENCE: Ourselves

▲ Name _____

A rainbow girl

You will need: a pencil; coloured pencils or crayons.

▲ Using coloured pencils or crayons, colour the drawing of a girl in the following way.
- Colour the hair red.
- Colour the arms orange.
- Colour the hands yellow.
- Colour the body green.
- Colour the legs blue.
- Colour the feet purple.

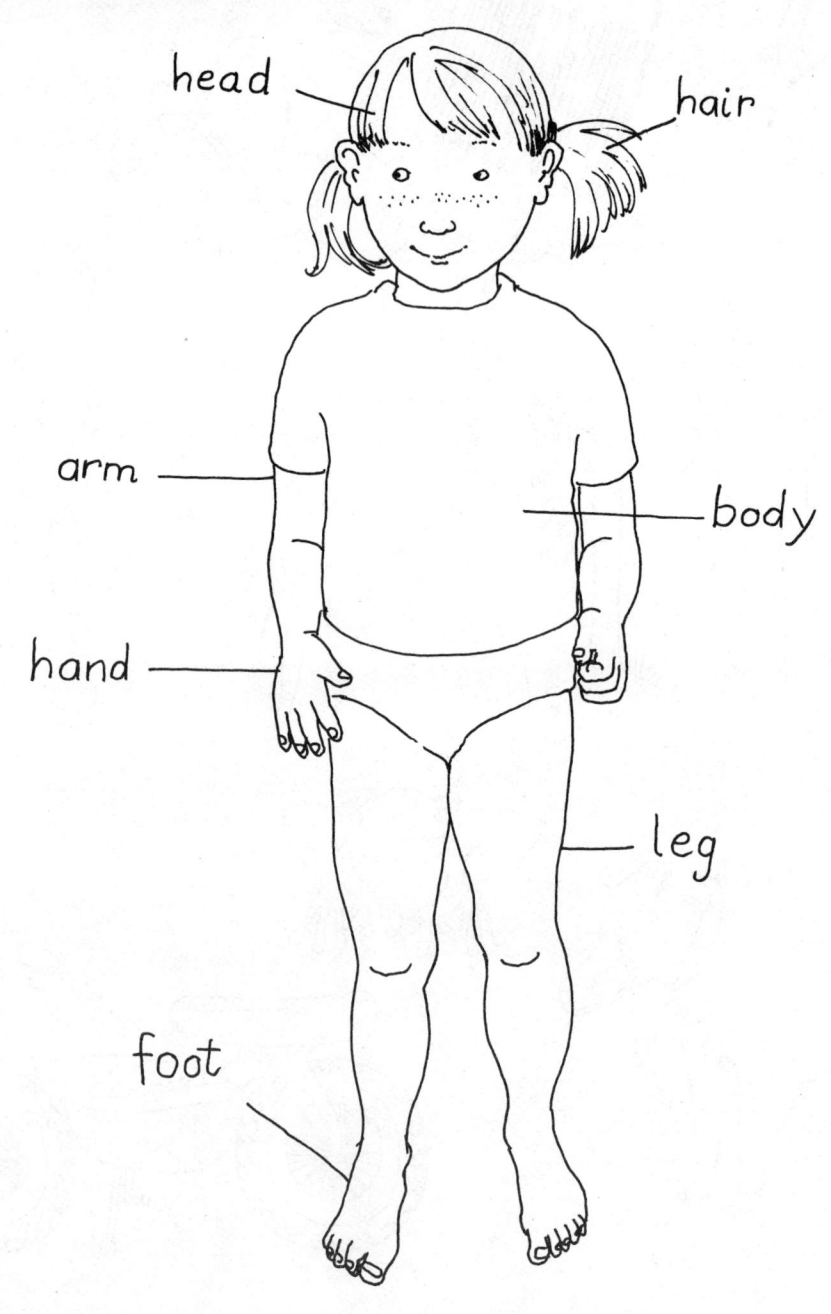

▲ Now draw and colour a rainbow boy.

▲ ESSENTIALS FOR SCIENCE: Ourselves

▲ Name _____

A body game

You will need: a toy brick; small pictures of parts of the body; glue; a pencil.

Work with some friends.

▲ Stick a small picture on each side of the brick. Then roll the brick. Can your friend name the part of the body that lands face up? Now try this with other friends. Who knows the most parts of the body?

▲ Draw a picture of yourself. Label the parts of your body.

▲ ESSENTIALS FOR SCIENCE: Ourselves

▲ Name _____

Body measurements

You will need: a tape measure; a pencil.

Work with a friend.

▲ Measure how tall you are.   I am _____ cm high.

▲ Measure your hand-span.   My hand-span is _____ cm.

▲ Measure your foot.   My foot is _____ cm long.

▲ Measure your arm-span.   My arm-span is _____ cm.

▲ Now measure your friend. Are your friend's measurements the same as yours?

▲ ESSENTIALS FOR SCIENCE: Ourselves

▲ Name _____

What I can do with my body

You will need: a pencil.

▲ Look at these pictures. Say which part of your body you use for each of these activities. Choose from: hands, legs, head, eyes, ears and your whole body.

▲ ESSENTIALS FOR SCIENCE: Ourselves   9

▲ Name _____

Your weight

You will need: bathroom scales; a pencil.

▲ When you were born you weighed about 4 kilogrammmes. How much do you weigh now? Stand on the scales and see.

▲ Write it like this: I weigh _____ kilogrammes.

▲ Who in your class weighs more than you?
Who weighs less than you?

These weigh less then me:		These weigh more then me:	
Name	Weight	Name	Weight
_____	_____	_____	_____
_____	_____	_____	_____
_____	_____	_____	_____
_____	_____	_____	_____
_____	_____	_____	_____

▲ ESSENTIALS FOR SCIENCE: Ourselves

▲ Name _____

Your face

You will need: a mirror; a pencil.

▲ Look at your face in the mirror. Draw your face in this shape.

▲ Label as many parts as you can.

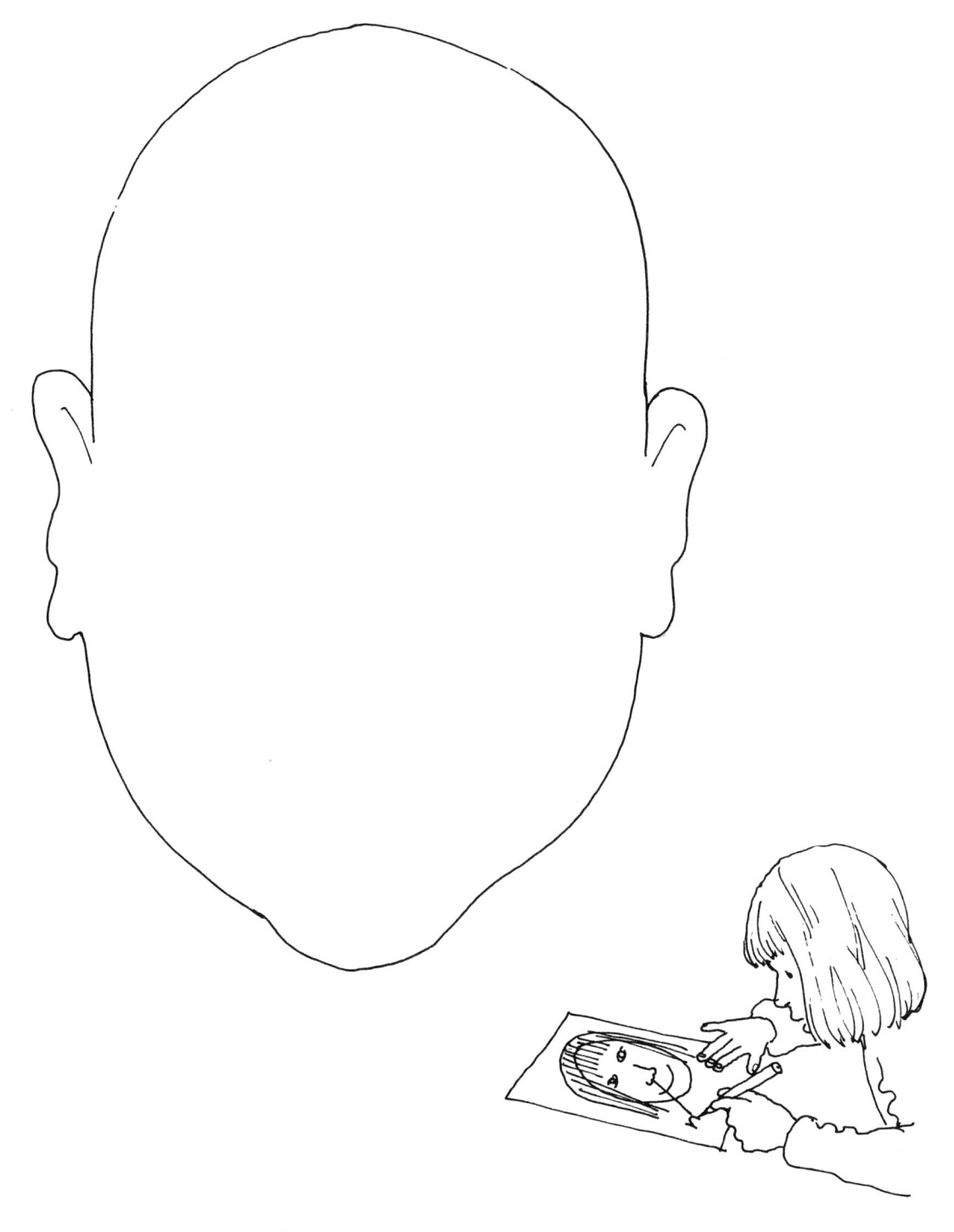

▲ Draw how you would look if you were happy, sad, angry or surprised.

▲ ESSENTIALS FOR SCIENCE: Ourselves

▲ Name _____

Make face masks

You will need: paper plates; sticks; glue; a pencil; coloured pencils or crayons.

▲ Draw some faces on the plates.

▲ Glue two plates together with the stick wedged between them.

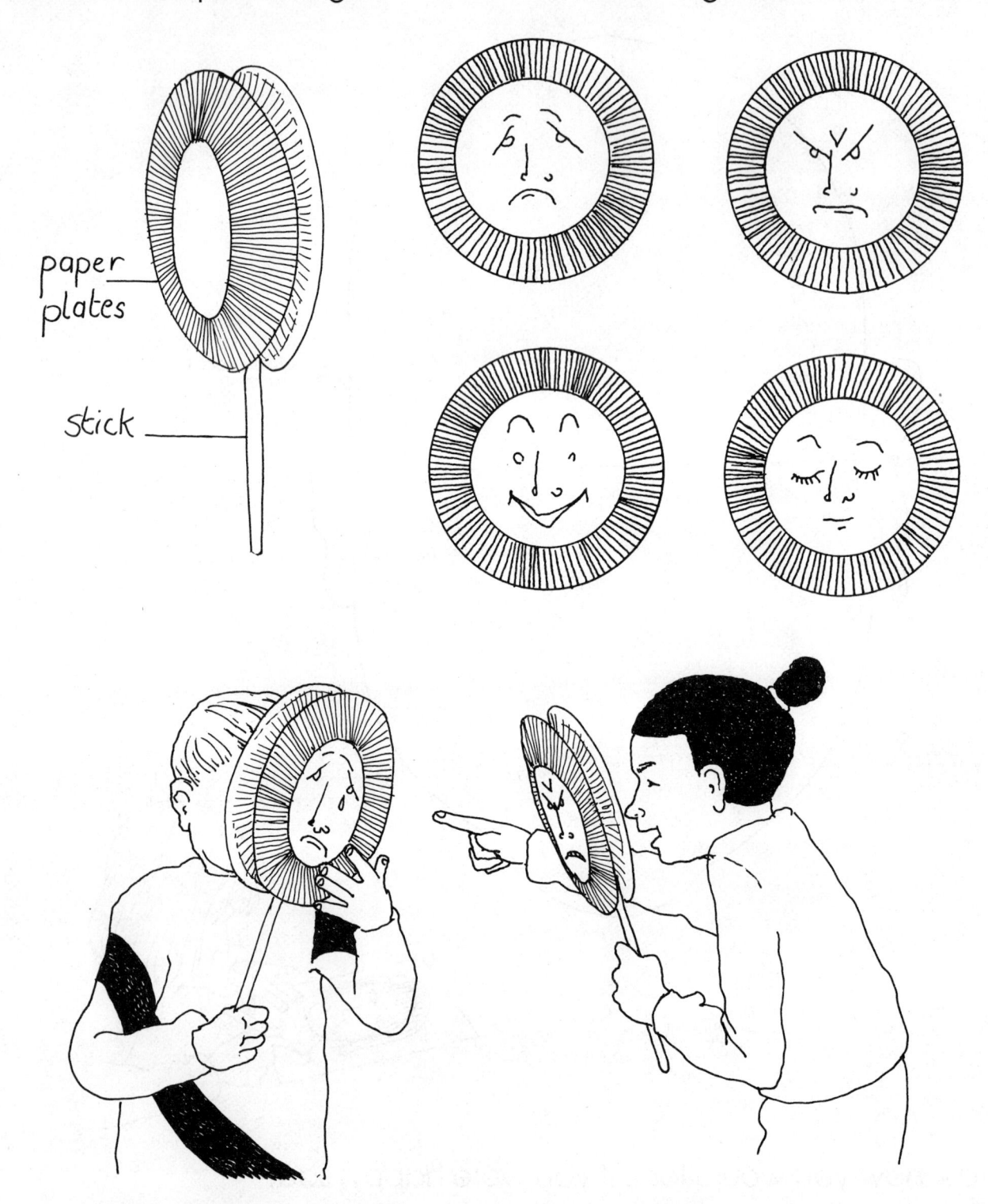

▲ Make a mask play. Tell the story using the right faces.

ESSENTIALS FOR SCIENCE: Ourselves

▲ Name _____

Hair

You will need: a long hair; sticky tape; paper; paper-clips; a pencil.

▲ What colour is your hair? Is it brown, black, red or fair?

My hair is _____

▲ How strong is a hair? Fix a long hair like in the picture below with a paper loop on the end. Put paper-clips, one at a time, into the loop of paper attached to the hair.

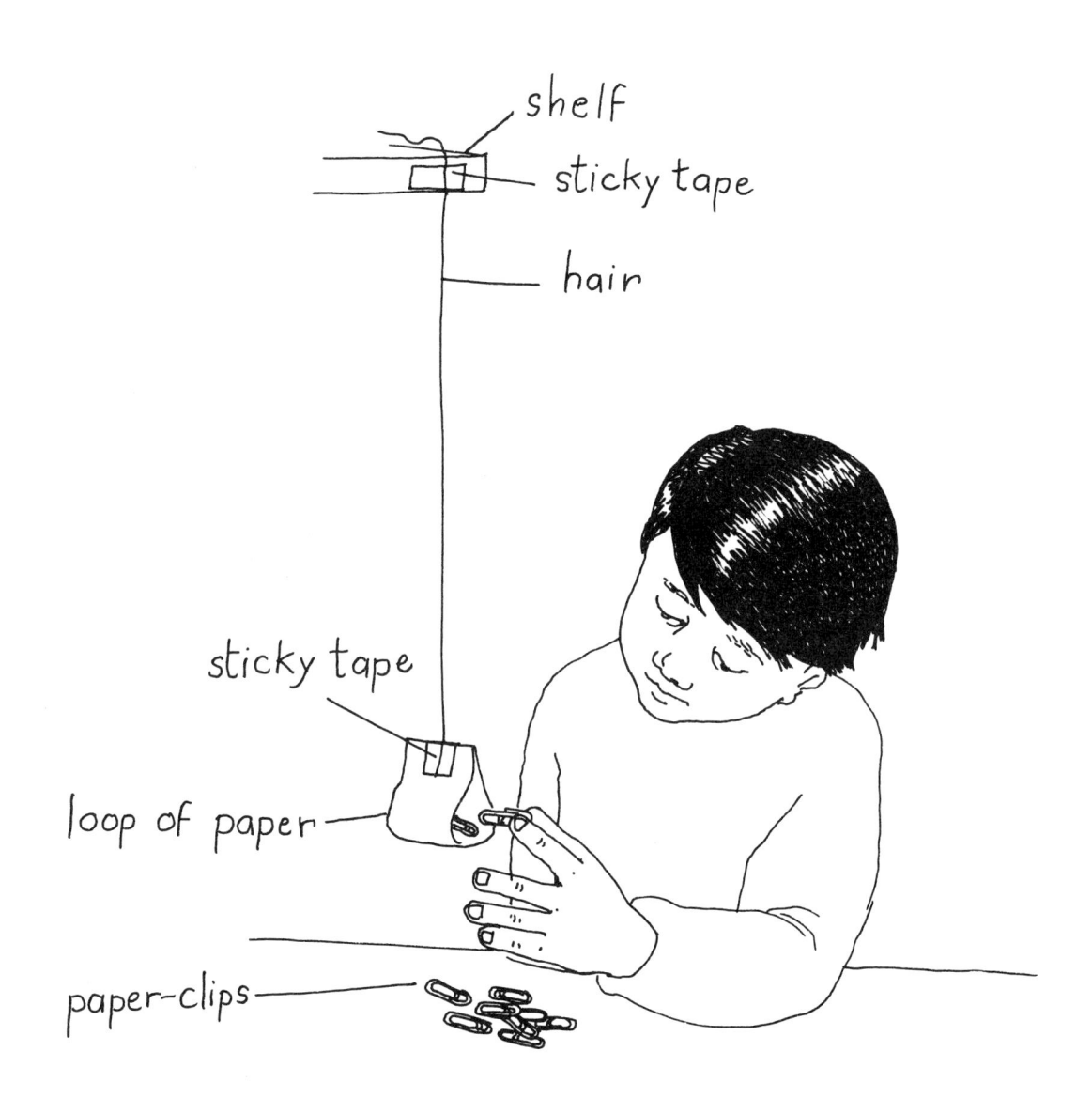

▲ Try this again with a hair from someone else.

▲ ESSENTIALS FOR SCIENCE: Ourselves

▲ Name _____

Your teeth

You will need: a small mirror; a chocolate biscuit; coloured pencils; a pencil.

▲ Look in the mirror at your teeth. Colour the tooth chart to show your teeth. How many teeth do you have altogether?

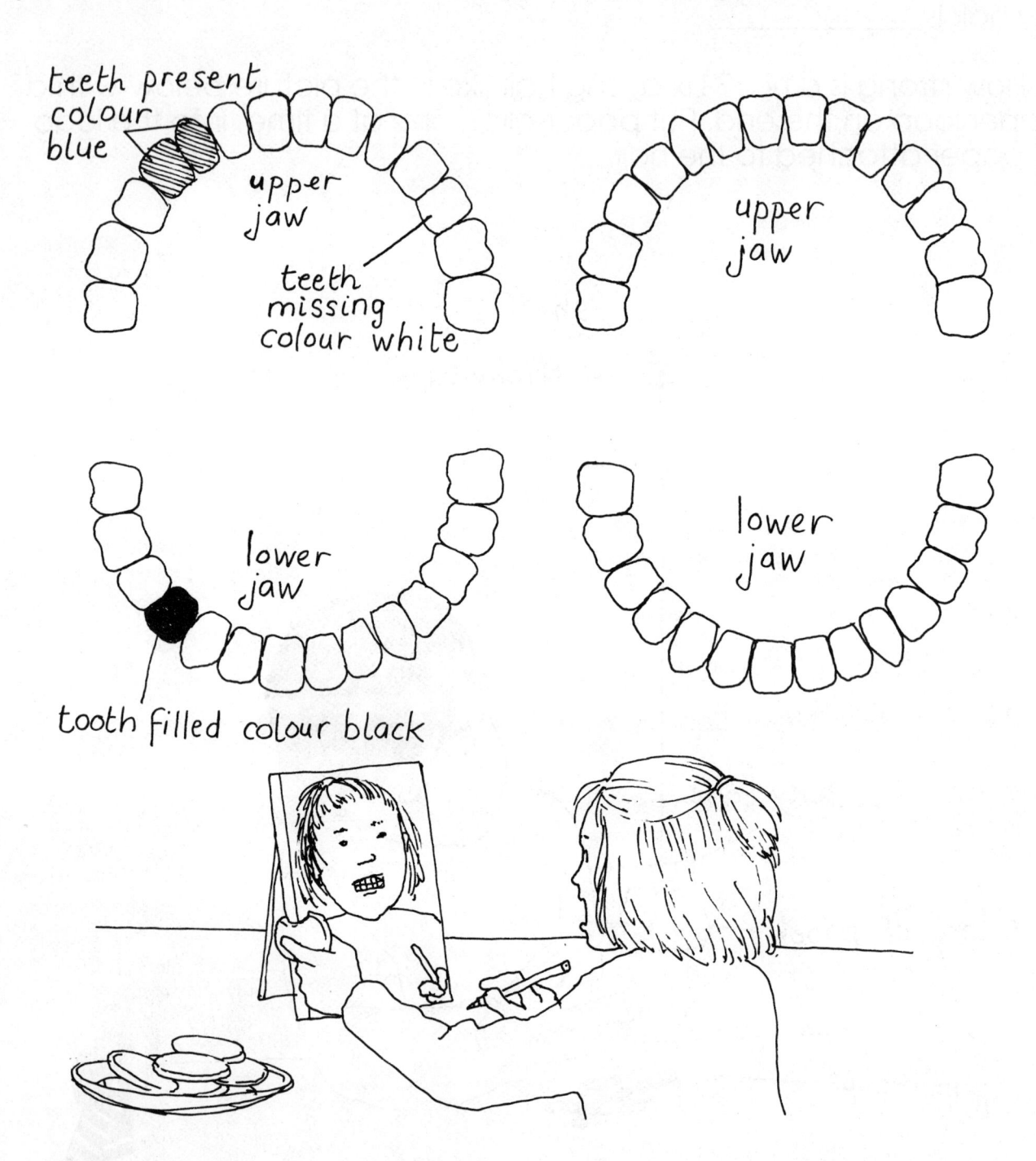

teeth present colour blue

upper jaw

teeth missing colour white

upper jaw

lower jaw

tooth filled colour black

lower jaw

▲ Chew the chocolate biscuit and look in the mirror. Where does the chocolate collect? Show these places on your chart.
▲ Why should we clean our teeth after meals?

▲ ESSENTIALS FOR SCIENCE: Ourselves

▲ Name _____

Senses

You will need: a pencil; a ruler.

▲ You have five senses. Match the sentence with the right part of the body.

- You see with your

- You hear with your

- You smell with your

- You touch with your

- You taste with your

▲ Which sense do you use most?

▲ Which senses do you use when eating your food?

▲ ESSENTIALS FOR SCIENCE: Ourselves

▲ Name _____

Tongues

You will need: a mirror; a pencil.

▲ Is everyone's tongue the same? Look in the mirror.
Is your tongue round or pointed?

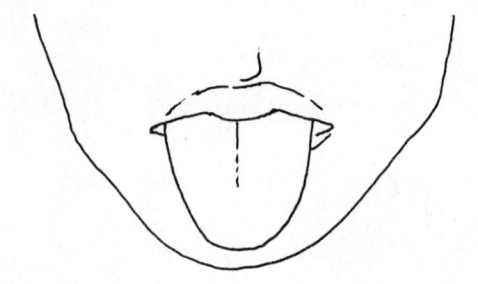

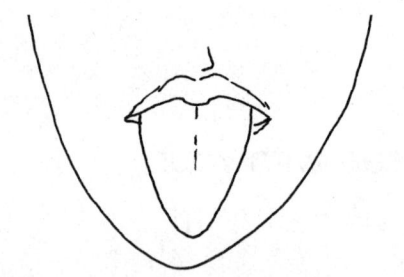

▲ Can you touch your nose with your tongue?

▲ Can you roll your tongue like this?

▲ Make a chart like this.
Say what your tongue and your friends' tongues are like.

Name	Round or pointed	Can roll tongue	Can touch nose with tongue

▲ ESSENTIALS FOR SCIENCE: Ourselves

▲ Name ______________________________

Eyes

You will need: a mirror; a pencil.

▲ Look in the mirror. Look at your eyes.

Can you see the parts shown in the picture?

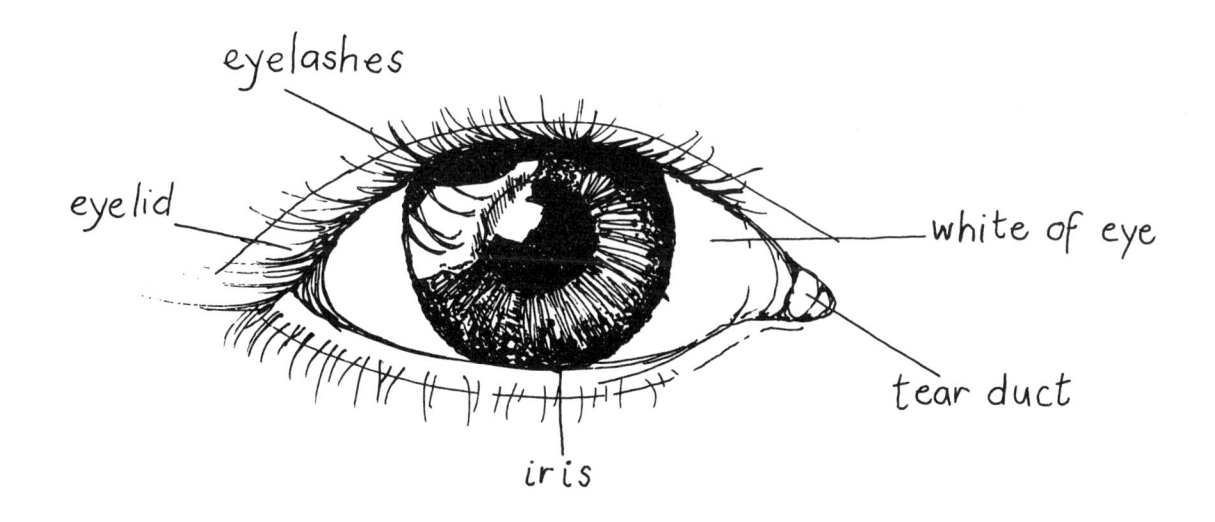

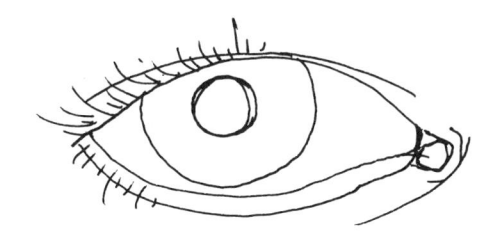

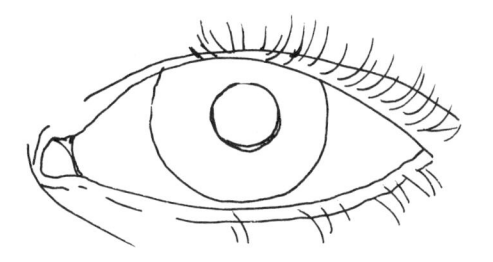

eyelashes
eyelid
white of eye
tear duct
iris

▲ Colour the picture.

▲ Are your friends' eyes the same colour as yours?

▲ Name _____

Can we believe our eyes?

You will need: a pencil; a ruler.

▲ Look carefully at the pictures. Can we always believe what we see?

Is this a vase? Or is it two faces?

Is this a rabbit? Or is it a duck?

Is this a young woman? Or is it an old woman?

Are there spots where the white lines cross?

Which flower centre is larger?

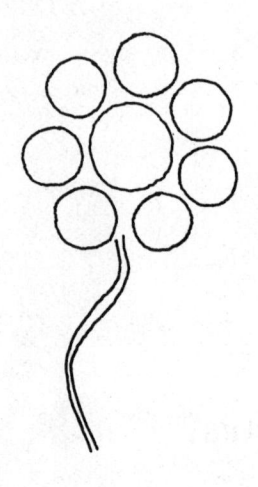

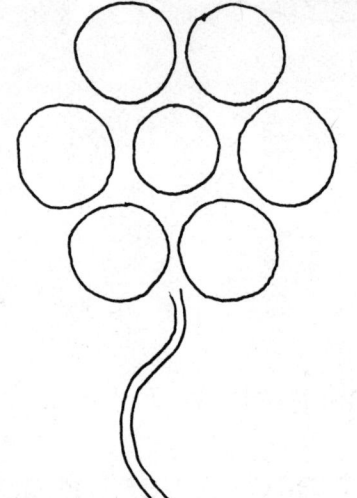

ESSENTIALS FOR SCIENCE: Ourselves

▲ Name _____

Food

You will need: a pencil; a ruler.

Some foods give us energy.   Some foods help to us grow.

Some foods keep us healthy.

▲ Which of these foods have you eaten today?
_____
_____

▲ Which foods do you like the best?
_____
_____

▲ Colour the foods that keep us healthy.

▲ ESSENTIALS FOR SCIENCE: Ourselves

▲ Name _____

Food from animals and plants

You will need: a pencil.

Some of our food comes from animals.

Some of our food comes from plants.

▲ Draw some more foods in each circle.

▲ ESSENTIALS FOR SCIENCE: Ourselves

▲ Name _____

The skeleton

You will need: a tape measure.

▲ Look at this picture of a skeleton. It is made up of bones.
▲ Can you feel your bones?
▲ Measure some of your bones.

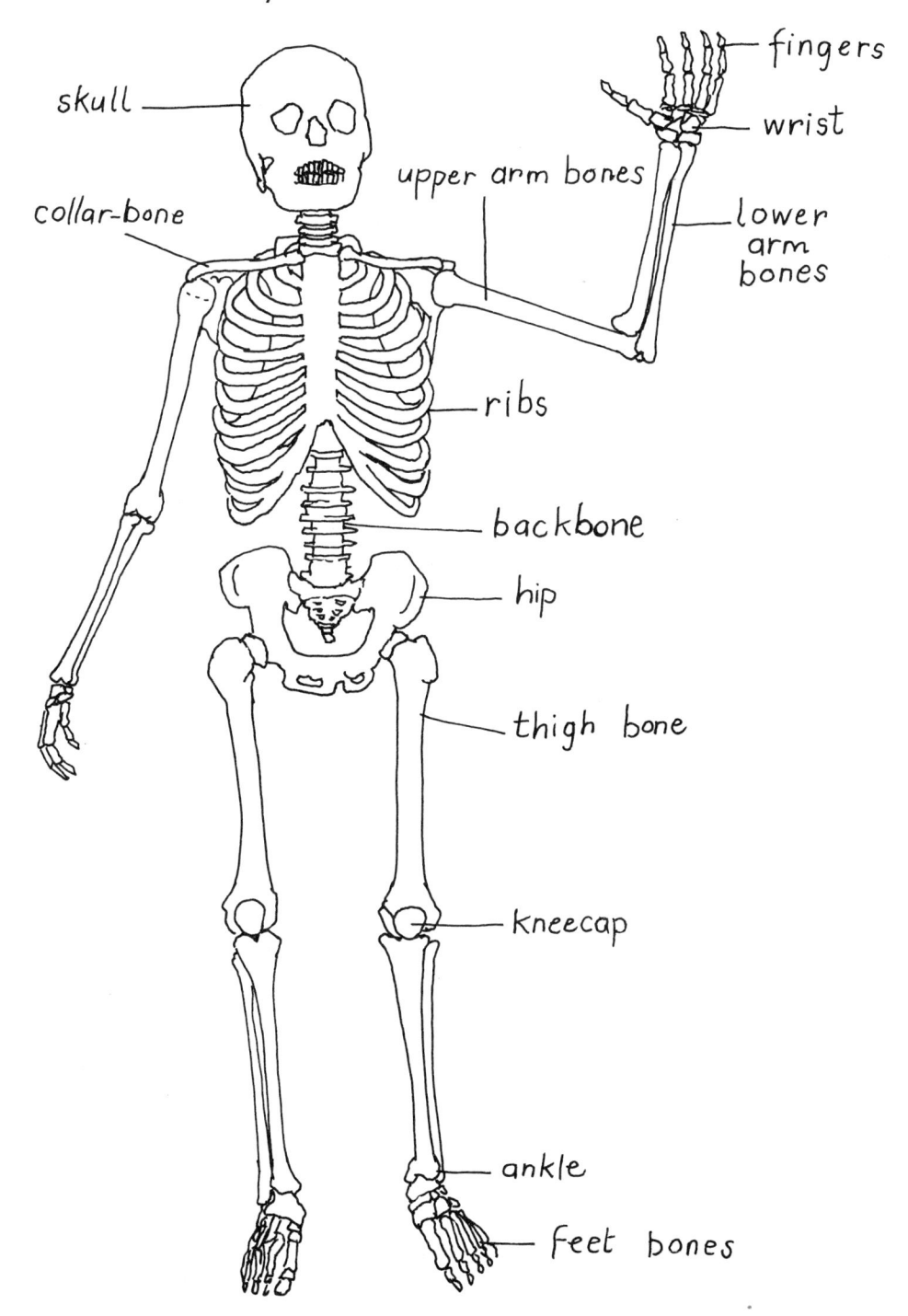

- skull
- collar-bone
- upper arm bones
- fingers
- wrist
- lower arm bones
- ribs
- backbone
- hip
- thigh bone
- kneecap
- ankle
- feet bones

▲ Which is the longest bone you can find? Which is the shortest?

▲ ESSENTIALS FOR SCIENCE: Ourselves

▲ Name _____

Joints

You will need: thin card; scissors; paper fasteners; glue.

We can move because we have joints. Joints are places where two bones meet.

▲ Make this jointed figure. Stick the shapes below on to thin card. Carefully cut out the shapes. Make small holes in each part as shown. Join the parts with paper fasteners. Play with your jointed figure.

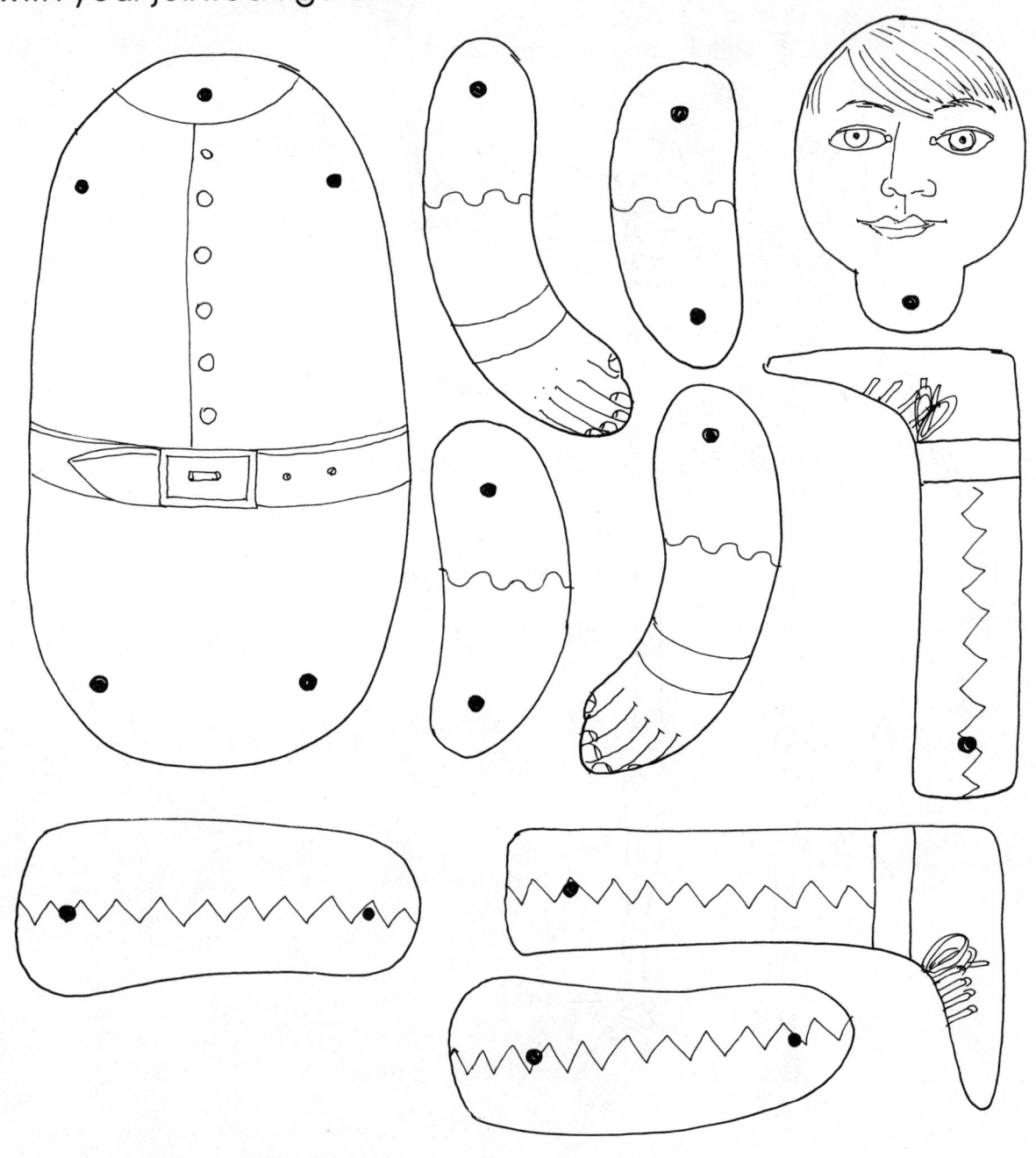

▲ How many of these joints can you find on your body?
▲ Are there any joints on your body which are not on the figure?

▲ ESSENTIALS FOR SCIENCE: Ourselves

▲ Name _____

Listen to your heartbeat

You will need: a tube; two plastic funnels; a pencil.

▲ Put the funnels in the tube like this. Listen to your heartbeat. Run around the playground. Listen again. Sit still and listen again. What do you notice?

plastic or rubber tube

funnel

▲ ESSENTIALS FOR SCIENCE: Ourselves

▲ Name _____

Breathing

⚠

You will need: a pencil.

Living things breathe. They need air to stay alive. You breathe all the time. You breathe air to keep you alive.

▲ Put your hands on your chest. Breathe in. Can you feel your chest move? Breathe out. Can you feel your chest move?

▲ Now run around the playground. Put your hands on your chest again. Do you breathe faster or slower? How can you find out?

▲ ESSENTIALS FOR SCIENCE: Ourselves

▲ Name _____

Growing

You will need: a pencil.

As we grow, we get bigger. It takes time to grow.

▲ Look at these children.

Caroline is 6 months old.
Petra is 6 years old.
Kevin is 14 years old.
Sanjit is 1 year old.
Kirsty is 2 years old.

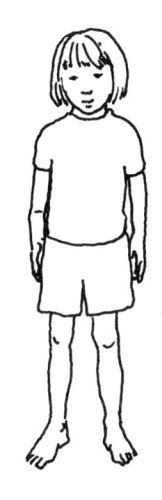

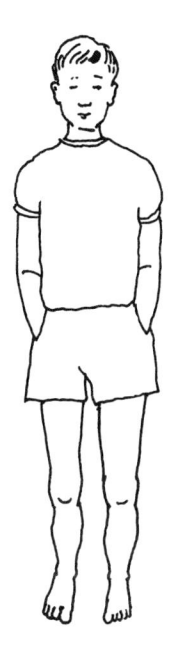

▲ Write each of the children's names under their picture.

▲ Draw some of the clothes Caroline might wear.
▲ Draw some of the clothes Petra might wear.

▲ ESSENTIALS FOR SCIENCE: Ourselves

▲ Name _____

You as a baby

You will need: a pencil.

▲ Find out all you can about yourself when you were a baby.

When were you born? _____

Where were you born? _____

How much did you weigh? _____

What was your hair like? _____

When did you first walk? _____

What was your first word? _____

What toys did you play with? _____

Have you a picture of yourself when you were a baby?

▲ ESSENTIALS FOR SCIENCE: Ourselves

▲ Name _____

Me and my friends

You will need: a pencil; a tape measure; bathroom scales.

Work with some friends.

▲ Fill in this chart.

name	boy or girl	age	hair colour	height	weight

▲ Can you find anyone exactly like you?

▲ Name _____

How good is your memory?

You will need: a pencil; a clock with a second hand.

How much can you remember?

▲ Look carefully at this picture for one minute. Now cover the picture. How many of the things can you remember in two minutes? Write them down.

▲ Who has the best memory in your class?

▲ ESSENTIALS FOR SCIENCE: Ourselves

Which side of your body do you use the most?

You will need: a pen.

▲ Are you left-handed or right-handed? Pick up a pen and see.

▲ Scratch your back. Which hand do you use?

▲ Cup your hand to hear better. Which ear do you use?

▲ Wink at someone. Which eye do you use?

▲ Tilt your head on your shoulder. Which shoulder does your head touch?

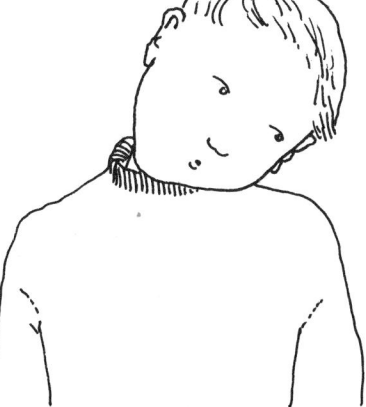

▲ ESSENTIALS FOR SCIENCE: Ourselves

▲ Name _____

Handprints

You will need: newspapers; a large, flat sponge; poster paint; paper; water; a pencil.

▲ Make some handprints. Mix the poster paint until it is runny. Soak the sponge on a thick layer of newspaper. Press your hand down on the sponge. Then press your hand on a clean sheet of paper.

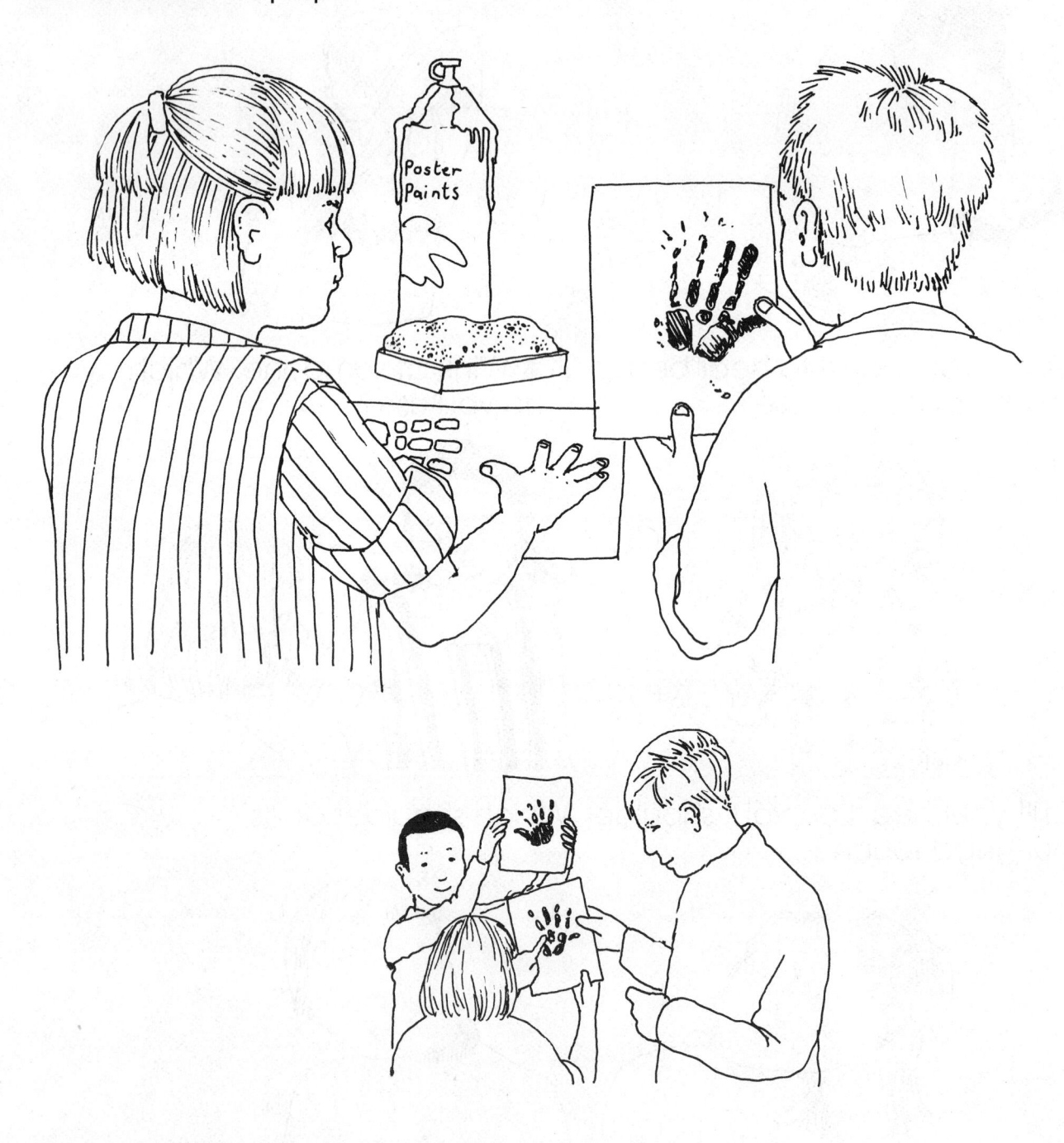

▲ Look at your handprint carefully. What do you notice?
▲ Is your handprint the same as those of your friends?

▲ ESSENTIALS FOR SCIENCE: Ourselves

▲ Name _____

Measuring hands

You will need: some squared paper; beads or marbles; a pencil.

▲ Put your hand on the paper. Draw round your hand. Count the squares in your hand picture. (Do not count very small parts of a square.)

Write down: My hand covers _____ squares.

▲ Here is another way of measuring your hand. See how many marbles you can pick up with it.

▲ Who has the biggest hands in your class? _____

▲ Whose hands are the smallest? _____

▲ ESSENTIALS FOR SCIENCE: Ourselves

▲ Name _____

All about me

You will need: a pencil; glue; scissors; paper.

▲ Make a book about yourself. Call it 'All about Me'. Stick some pictures of yourself in it. Put your fingerprints, handprints and footprints in it. Write down this information about yourself.

My height _____ My weight _____

The colour of my eyes _____ The colour of my hair _____

My favourite food _____ My favourite drink _____

My favourite animal _____ My favourite sport _____

My favourite television programme _____

My favourite colour _____

My favourite singer _____

▲ Compare your book with those of your friends. Is there anyone else exactly like you?

▲ ESSENTIALS FOR SCIENCE: Ourselves

Contents

Teachers' notes	1	Can sounds go along string?	18
Notes on individual activities	2	Make your own telephone	19
Everyday sounds	5	Your voice	20
Loud and soft sounds	6	Can you make your voice louder?	21
Sorting sounds	7	Musical instruments	22
High sounds and low sounds	8	Make a drum	23
Sound words	9	Make some maracas	24
What's that sound?	10	Make a guitar	25
Sounds from different surfaces	11	Bottle sounds	26
One ear or two?	12	Musical bottles	27
Make some paper ears	13	Sounds can bounce	28
Make a stethoscope	14	Making echoes	29
Balloon sounds	15	Sound messages	30
Feeling vibrations	16	Noise	31
Can you hear through wood?	17	Match the sounds	32

Teachers' notes

Aims of this book
▲ To examine the variety of sounds around us and to observe that they are produced by vibrations;
▲ To show some of the uses of sounds;
▲ To show how vibrations affect the loudness and softness of sounds;
▲ To show, simply, how our ears collect sounds;
▲ To show that echoes are reflected sounds;
▲ To examine some simple home-made musical instruments and to try to understand and change the sounds they make;
▲ To demonstrate that noise is unwanted sound.

Developing science skills

While it is not essential to follow the order of the worksheets, it is important that all those covering one aspect of the subject, such as musical instruments or echoes, are dealt with at approximately the same time.

Although it is in the *doing* of science that children learn best, this involves more than just practical work. As well as needing to observe, record, predict, measure, identify patterns, classify, explain and ask questions that can lead to further investigations, children need time to discuss their work. The worksheets should be discussed both before and after completion of the activity. This helps to clarify the main ideas and will help you to monitor progress and discover what interests the children, with a view to developing their interests in future sessions.

Scientific background

Sound
Everything that can be heard is a sound. Sound, like light and heat, is a form of energy that is caused by something moving and thus making the surrounding air move backwards and forwards (vibrate), often at speed. The vibrating particles of air (molecules) move closer together and then further apart. Sound waves, which are three-dimensional, are created when changes of air pressure spread out in all directions.

Ears and hearing
The outer ear is a flap, which acts as a sound-collecting trumpet. At the base of the ear canal is a stretched membrane, the ear-drum. This is set in motion by the vibrating air molecules close to it. The movements of the ear-drum are small, but are magnified by a system of three bony levers in the middle ear. The vibrations are transmitted to the inner ear which converts them into a nervous message. The brain receives these messages and interprets them as sounds.

How sound travels
Almost everything we hear has travelled through the air around us. Sound will travel through any material that can transmit vibrations: solids, liquids and gases, including air. Sound travels easily through wood and metal.

▲ ESSENTIALS FOR SCIENCE: Sound

Loudness and pitch

Sounds can differ in two important ways:
The *loudness* of a sound depends on the size (amplitude) of the vibrations making it. This in turn depends on the amount of energy needed to produce the vibrations. Also, the closer you are to the source of the sound, the louder it is.

The *pitch* of a sound depends on the rate of vibration of the object causing it. The number of vibrations in a second is called the frequency. The greater the frequency, the higher the pitch. A shrill, high note is produced by rapid vibrations; a deep, low note is produced by slow vibrations.

Echoes

Echoes are caused by the reflection of sound waves from large, smooth surfaces such as walls and cliffs. Big echoes can be avoided by designing buildings with no large, flat internal surfaces to reflect the sound, while smaller echoes (reverberations) can be prevented by covering surfaces with materials that absorb the sound energy such as carpets and peg board.

Musical instruments

Sound waves can be produced in several different ways, for example, by hitting, rubbing, plucking and blowing. To obtain musical notes, the frequency of the vibrations of the sound-producer must be changed. This can usually be done by altering the size, the tightness or the weight of the object which is vibrating. For example, the pitch of the note produced when one of the strings of a guitar vibrates depends on the length of the string, its thickness and its tension. The frequency of the vibration is higher (and the note has a higher pitch) when the string is shorter, thinner or tighter. In wind instruments, the length of the vibrating air column must be altered to change the pitch of the note.

Notes on individual activities

Page 5: Everyday sounds

Key idea: We hear a great variety of sounds every day. Some of them are loud, some are soft.
Extension: Classify sounds into those made by natural objects, such as plants and animals (including humans), and those made by machines and other man-made objects.

Page 6: Loud and soft sounds

Key idea: Sounds vary in loudness or softness.
Likely outcome: Loud sounds – motor cycle, drill, drum, bell; soft sounds – feather, butterfly, leaf, watch.
Extension: Investigate loud and soft sounds made by musical instruments.

Page 7: Sorting sounds

Key idea: There are various ways of sorting, or classifying, sounds and sound-producers.
Likely outcome: Other possible categories into which sound-producers can be placed include: winding (eg drill or hand-mixer) and rubbing (eg sandpaper).
Extension: Discuss the different sounds made by animals and the functions of the sounds.
Safety precautions: Ensure that sharp objects do not form part of the collection.

Page 8: High sounds and low sounds

Key idea: There are high sounds and low sounds.
Likely outcome: Some high sounds – whistle, triangle, alarm bell; some low sounds – drum, car horn, car or lorry engine, euphonium.
Extension: Identify high and low notes made by a piano or guitar.

Page 9: Sound words

Key idea: There is a great variety of both sounds and the words used to describe them.
Extension: Use 'sound' words in creative writing.

Page 10: What's that sound?

Key idea: It is difficult to identify sounds but the ability improves with practice.
Extension: Use a tape-recorder to record common sounds for the children to identify.

Page 11: Sounds from different surfaces

Key idea: The same object, dropped from the same height, makes different sounds according to the type of surface it falls on.
Likely outcome: The loudest sound will come from a hard surface such as concrete or ceramic tiles. The softest sound will be on a soft, absorbent surface such as carpet or carpet tiles.
Extension: Experiment with listening to a soft sound, such as a pin dropped on to a metal tray from a fixed height, at varying distances.

Page 12: One ear or two?

Key idea: Having two ears enables us to locate the direction from which sounds are coming.
Likely outcome: It is easier to tell where sounds are coming from if both ears are used.
Extension: Devise and experiment with simple hearing tests. Discuss hearing and deafness.

Page 13: Make some paper ears

Key ideas: The larger the outer ear, the softer the sounds it can pick up.
Likely outcome: It is possible to hear better with larger outer ears.
Extension: Cup the hands in front of the ears, with the palms pointing backwards, to listen to soft sounds from behind you.

Page 14: Make a stethoscope
Key idea: A funnel shape will pick up soft sounds and transmit them to the ear so that they can be heard more easily.
Likely outcome: It is possible to hear one's own heartbeat or the ticking of a watch quite clearly with the model stethoscope.
Extension: Listen to the heartbeat before and after mild exercise.
Safety precautions: Do not let the children put the end of the tube in their ears.

Page 15: Balloon sounds
Key idea: The mouth of a balloon will vibrate, as air passes over it quickly, producing sounds.
Likely outcome: The sound the balloon makes can be varied by stretching or relaxing its mouth.
Extension: Discuss the sounds made by strong winds blowing through trees or telephone wires. Use an inflated balloon to blow through a whistle.
Safety precaution: Do not release air from the balloon close to the face.

Page 16: Feeling vibrations
Key idea: Sounds make an inflated balloon vibrate.
Likely outcome: Soft sounds make the balloon vibrate slightly, loud sounds make it vibrate a lot.
Extension: Compare the vibrating balloon with the vibration of the ear-drum.
Safety precautions: Use a small, battery operated radio, not one using mains electricity.

Page 17: Can you hear through wood?
Key idea: Sounds pass more easily through wood than they do through air.
Likely outcome: Soft sounds can be heard more easily through wood than they can through air. Metals also transmit sounds better than air.
Extension: Can sounds pass through water? Listen to a ticking watch through an inflated balloon and then through the balloon filled with water.

Page 18: Can sounds go along string?
Key idea: Sounds can pass along string.
Likely outcome: Faint sounds made by tapping the spoons together can be heard quite clearly.
Extension: Discuss why North American Indians used to put their ears to the ground to listen for the sounds of distant hoofbeats.

Page 19: Make your own telephone
Key idea: Sounds can travel through taut string.
Likely outcome: Sounds will travel along the string when it is taut, but not when it hangs down loosely. If additional pots and string are added, to work effectively all the string must be kept taut. (A real telephone works because sounds cause pulses of electricity to pass along the wire from the transmitting instrument to the receiving one.)

Page 20: Your voice
Key idea: The voice comes from the voice box which is in the throat.
Likely outcome: The children will feel their voice box or 'Adam's apple' moving while they are talking, shouting and singing.

Page 21: Can you make your voice louder?
Key ideas: Sounds travel out in a wide arc from the mouth. They can be made to travel further if they are directed with a funnel-shaped object.
Likely outcome: The sounds will travel further if they are directed by the model megaphone.

Page 22: Musical instruments
Key idea: Three main ways in which musical instruments work is by blowing, plucking and banging (or tapping).
Likely outcome: Blowing – recorder, trumpet; plucking – guitar, harp; banging – cymbals, piano.
Extension: Make a model xylophone using different-sized blocks of wood, or different-sized clay plant pots suspended by string from a long stick. Tap them with a metal spoon.

Page 23: Make a drum
Key idea: The skin of the drum vibrates when it makes a sound.
Likely outcome: When the drum is tapped the rice grains bounce up and down, showing that it is the skin of the drum which vibrates. This makes the air inside the drum vibrate to make a sound.

Page 24: Make some maracas
Key idea: Maracas and other percussion instruments consist of small objects vibrating inside a box-type structure.
Likely outcome: It is the vibration of the peas, rice or small stones which makes the sounds.

Page 25: Make a guitar
Key ideas: The sound made by a vibrating rubber band varies according to its thickness. If a rubber band vibrates over a box-like structure, it will make a louder sound.
Likely outcome: In general, the thinner rubber bands will make higher notes than the thicker ones, assuming they are all under approximately the same degree of tension. When the tension is increased, they will make a higher note.
Safety precautions: Warn the children of the dangers to the face and eyes from over-stretched rubber bands.

Page 26: Bottle sounds
Key idea: A column of air can vibrate to make a sound.

Likely outcome: The note made by blowing over the top of the bottles varies according to the size of bottle. It is the air in the bottles which is vibrating, not the glass or plastic from which they are made.
Safety precautions: Use care with glass bottles.

Page 27: Musical bottles

Key idea: By varying the height of the column of air in a row of bottles, it is possible to produce a range of musical notes.
Likely outcome: A succession of notes can be played if each of the bottles is struck in turn with the spoon.
Safety precautions: Use care with glass bottles.

Page 28: Sounds can bounce

Key idea: Sounds can bounce (or be reflected) off a smooth, hard surface.
Likely outcome: The watch cannot be heard ticking until the plate is held near the far ends of the tubes. The sound travels up the tube containing the watch, is reflected by the plate and travels down the other tube to the ear.
Extension: Replace the plate in this activity with other soft and hard materials. See which reflect the sound and which absorb it. Make echoes in an uncarpeted hall or corridor.

Page 29: Making echoes

Key idea: A curved surface such as a bucket can produce a whole series of small echoes.
Likely outcome: It is difficult to speak into a bucket because a series of small echoes (called reverberations) are reflected back to the ears of the speaker.

Page 30: Sound messages

Key idea: Sounds can be used to give warnings or messages.
Likely outcome: Bell – doorbell, telephone, alarm clock, school bell; siren – ambulance, fire engine; whistle – kettle, referee.
Extension: Discuss the use of warning sounds at, for example, pedestrian road crossings.

Page 31: Noise

Key ideas: We call unpleasant sounds noise. It is possible to reduce noise by various sound-insulation materials.
Likely outcome: The cardboard box may reduce the sound of the radio slightly, but the newspaper can reduce the sound considerably, as can other soft materials such as cotton wool, woollen cloth and polystyrene beads.
Extension: Discuss the implications for road safety of wearing headphones or coats with hoods.

Page 32: Match the sounds

Key idea: Different animals (including the human animal) make different sounds.
Likely outcome: Baby crying – Boo hoo! Cow – Moo! Horse – Clip-clop! Bee – Buzz! Dog – Woof! Cat – Miaow!
Extension: Discuss which sounds are pleasant/unpleasant; easiest/hardest to hear. Why?

National Curriculum: Science

In addition to the PoS for AT1, the following PoS are relevant to this book:

AT2 – Pupils should:
• find out about themselves and develop their ideas about how they grow, feed, move, use their senses and about the stages of human development (i)
• consider similarities and differences between themselves and other pupils and understand that individuals are unique. (ii)

AT4 – Pupils should:
• have the opportunity to experience the range of sounds in their immediate environment and to find out about their causes and effects. They should experience the production of echoes resulting from the reflection of sound from distant surfaces. They should explore how to make and experience sounds by speaking and singing, striking, plucking, shaking, scraping and blowing, using familiar objects and simple musical instruments from a variety of cultural traditions. (iv)

Scottish 5-14 Curriculum

Environmental studies
Attainment outcomes: Science in the environment (sound)
Healthy and safe living (the senses)
Investigating (finding out, interpreting)
Designing and making (plan, make, evaluate, present)

Expressive arts: music
Attainment outcomes: Using materials (exploring sound, using instruments)
Evaluating and appreciating (observing, listening, responding)

▲ ESSENTIALS FOR SCIENCE: Sound

▲ Name _____

Everyday sounds

▲ Listen carefully. What sounds can you hear?
▲ Are they loud or soft sounds?
▲ Fill in the table of sounds.

Loud sounds	Soft sounds
motorbike	whisper

▲ Which sound do you like best? _____
▲ Why? _____

▲ ESSENTIALS FOR SCIENCE: Sound

▲ Name _____

Loud and soft sounds

▲ Do the things below make loud sounds or soft sounds?
▲ Write or draw them in the right box.

Loud sounds		Soft sounds

▲ Think of some other objects that make loud or soft sounds.
▲ Write their names in the boxes.

▲ ESSENTIALS FOR SCIENCE: Sound

▲ Name _____

Sorting sounds

You will need: five boxes; things that make sounds.

▲ Collect some things that make sounds. Which box should each one go in?

[boxes labeled: blow, pluck, shake, bang, scrape]

▲ Do you need any more boxes?
▲ How else could you sort the sounds?

▲ ESSENTIALS FOR SCIENCE: Sound

▲ Name _____

High sounds and low sounds

▲ Make a squeak like a mouse. That is a high sound.
▲ Make a noise like a car engine. That is a low sound.
▲ Listen. How many high sounds can you hear now?
▲ Listen. How many low sounds can you hear now?
▲ Write them in the boxes.

High sounds	Low sounds

▲ ESSENTIALS FOR SCIENCE: Sound

▲ Name _____

Sound words

Here are some sound words.

splash   bang   rustle   tick

▲ Put the right word by the picture.

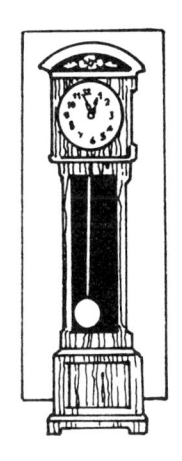

▲ Write down some more sound words. Draw a picture below for one of them.

▲ ESSENTIALS FOR SCIENCE: Sound

▲ Name _____

What's that sound?

You will need: a friend to work with; pebble; button; bead; marble; dried peas; clothes peg; small pencil; paper clip; a box with a lid.

▲ Can you tell one sound from another?
▲ Ask your friend to close his or her eyes.
▲ Put a small object in the box. Shake it.

▲ Ask your friend to say what is in the box.
▲ Now try other objects.
▲ Can you do better than your friend?
▲ Which made the quietest noise?
▲ Which made the loudest noise?

▲ ESSENTIALS FOR SCIENCE: Sound

▲ Name _____

Sounds from different surfaces

You will need: a coin; a ruler.

▲ Drop a coin on the table.

▲ Drop a coin on the floor.

▲ Drop a coin on the carpet.

▲ When does the coin make a loud sound?
▲ When does the coin make a soft sound?
▲ Cut out the pictures above and put them in order with the loudest first.

▲ ESSENTIALS FOR SCIENCE: Sound

▲ Name _____

One ear or two?

You will need: a friend to work with; a triangle.

▲ Listen with one ear. Close your eyes. Point to the sound.

▲ Listen with two ears. Close your eyes. Point to the sound. Are two ears better than one?

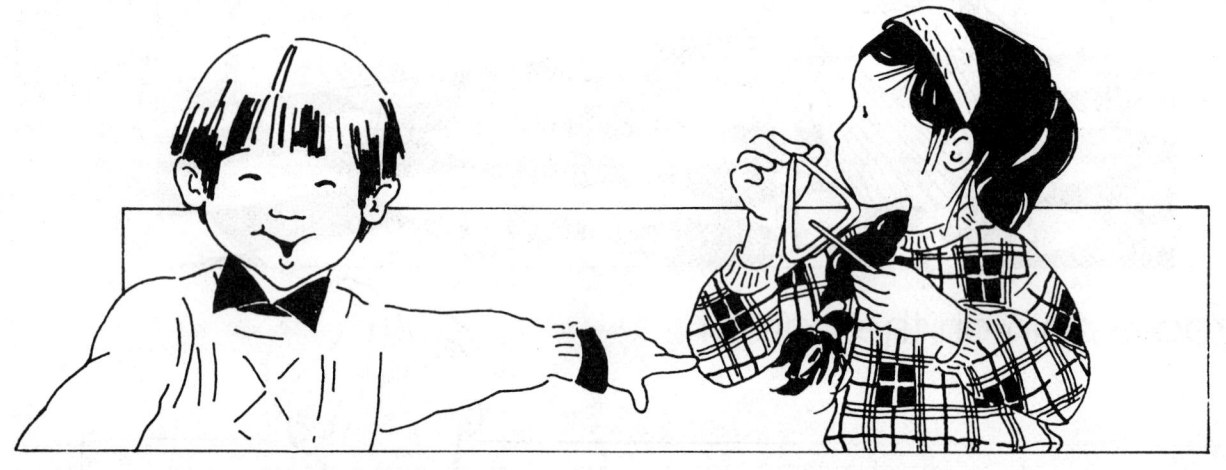

▲ Draw an animal using his ears to listen with.

▲ ESSENTIALS FOR SCIENCE: Sound

▲ Name _____

Make some paper ears

You will need: some thick paper; scissors; sticky tape.

▲ Make some paper ears. Put them over your ears.
▲ Can you hear better with the paper ears?
▲ Can you hear better without the paper ears?

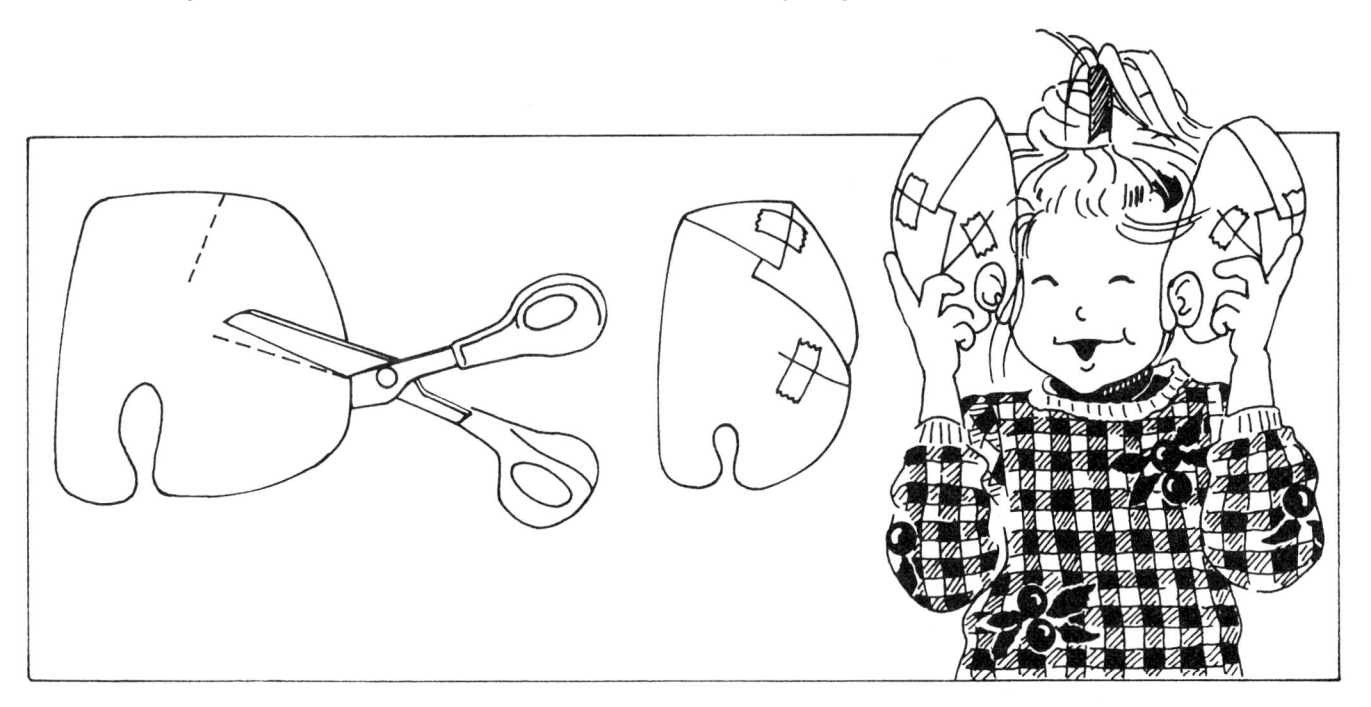

▲ Which animals do you know that have large ears?
▲ Draw some of them and write their names.

▲ ESSENTIALS FOR SCIENCE: Sound

▲ Name _____

Make a stethoscope

You will need: a plastic tube; two funnels.

The doctor listens to soft sounds.
She listens with a stethoscope.

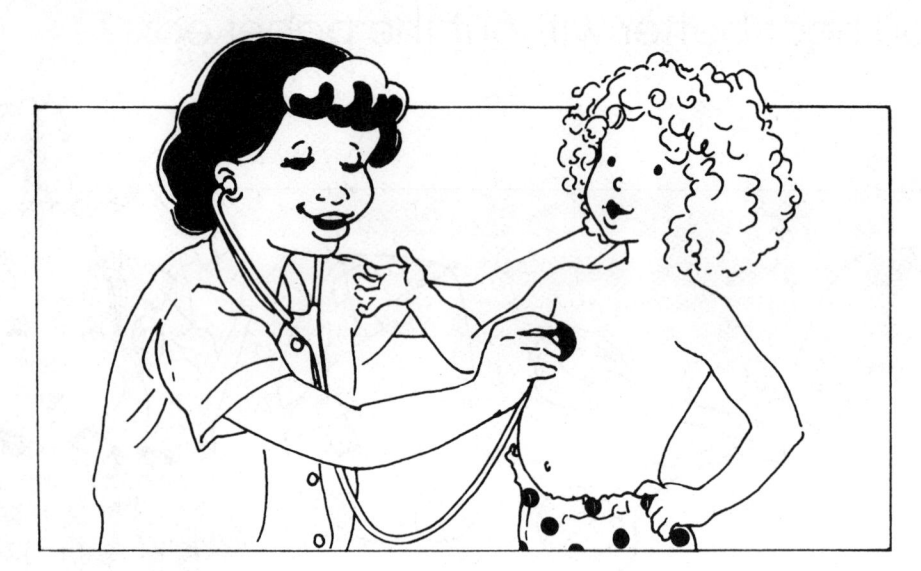

▲ Make your own stethoscope.

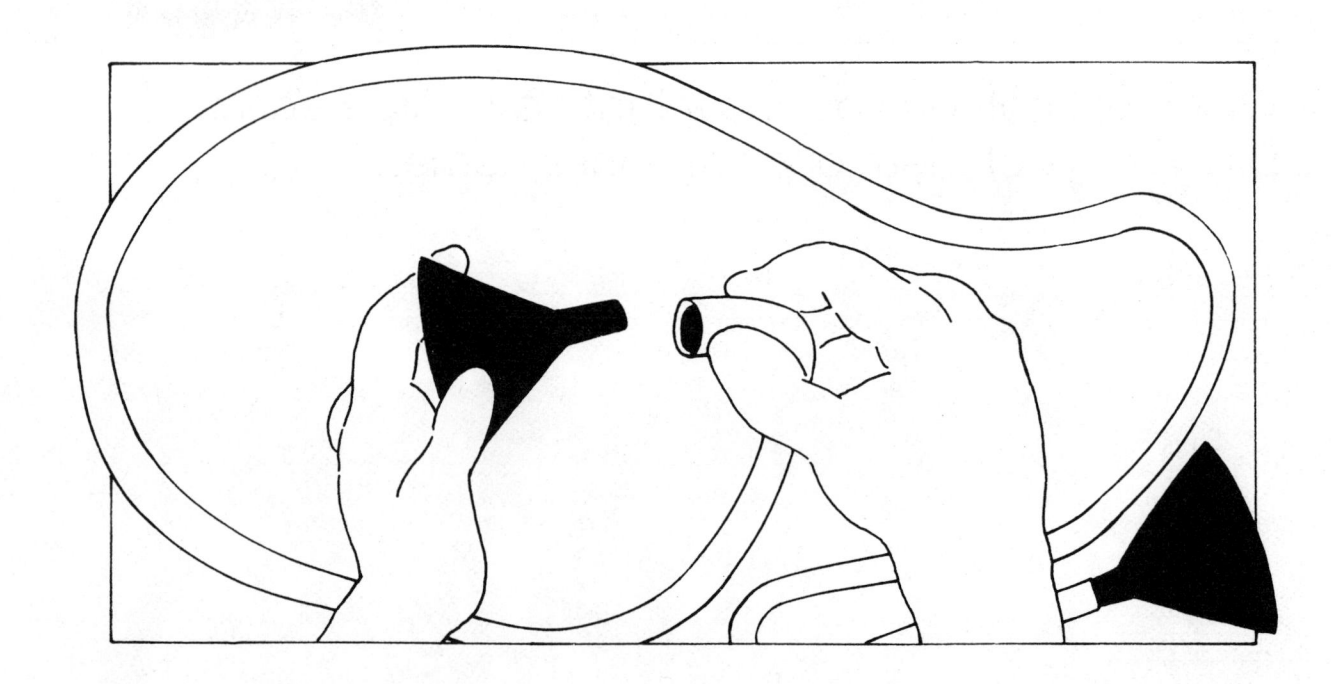

▲ What soft sounds can you hear with it?
▲ Make a list of the sounds you can hear.
▲ Can you hear soft sounds with a cardboard tube?

▲ ESSENTIALS FOR SCIENCE: Sound

▲ Name _____

Balloon sounds

You will need: a balloon.

▲ Ask an adult to blow up the balloon for you. Hold the balloon like this.

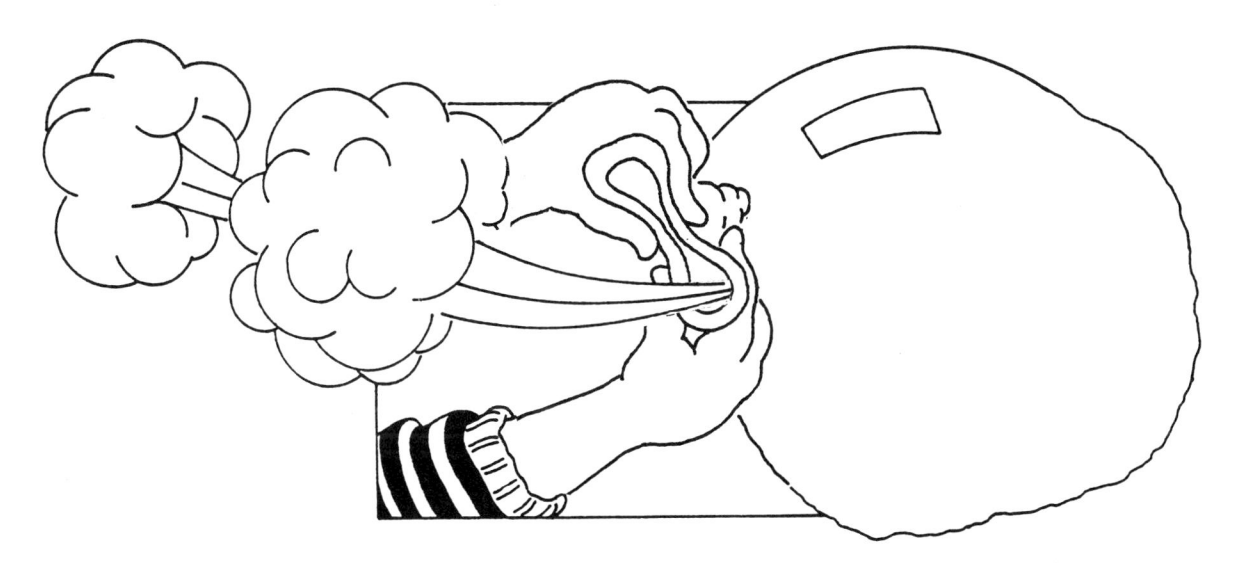

▲ Can you see the mouth of the balloon moving?
▲ What sound does the balloon make?
▲ Will your balloon make other sounds?
▲ Draw a picture or write about the sound a balloon can make.

▲ ESSENTIALS FOR SCIENCE: Sound

▲ Name _____

Feeling vibrations

You will need: a blown-up balloon.

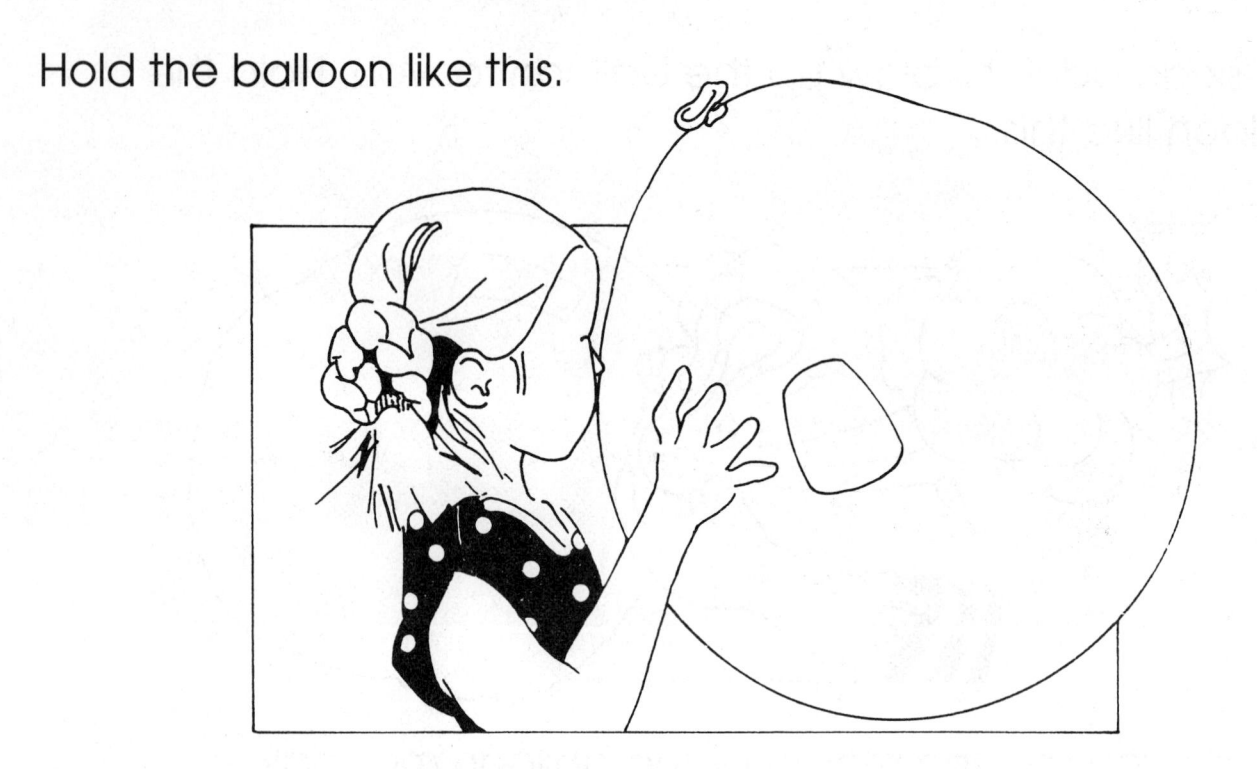

Hold the balloon like this.

▲ Talk. What do you feel?
▲ Shout. What do you feel?
▲ What happens when you sing?
▲ What happens if you put the balloon near a radio?

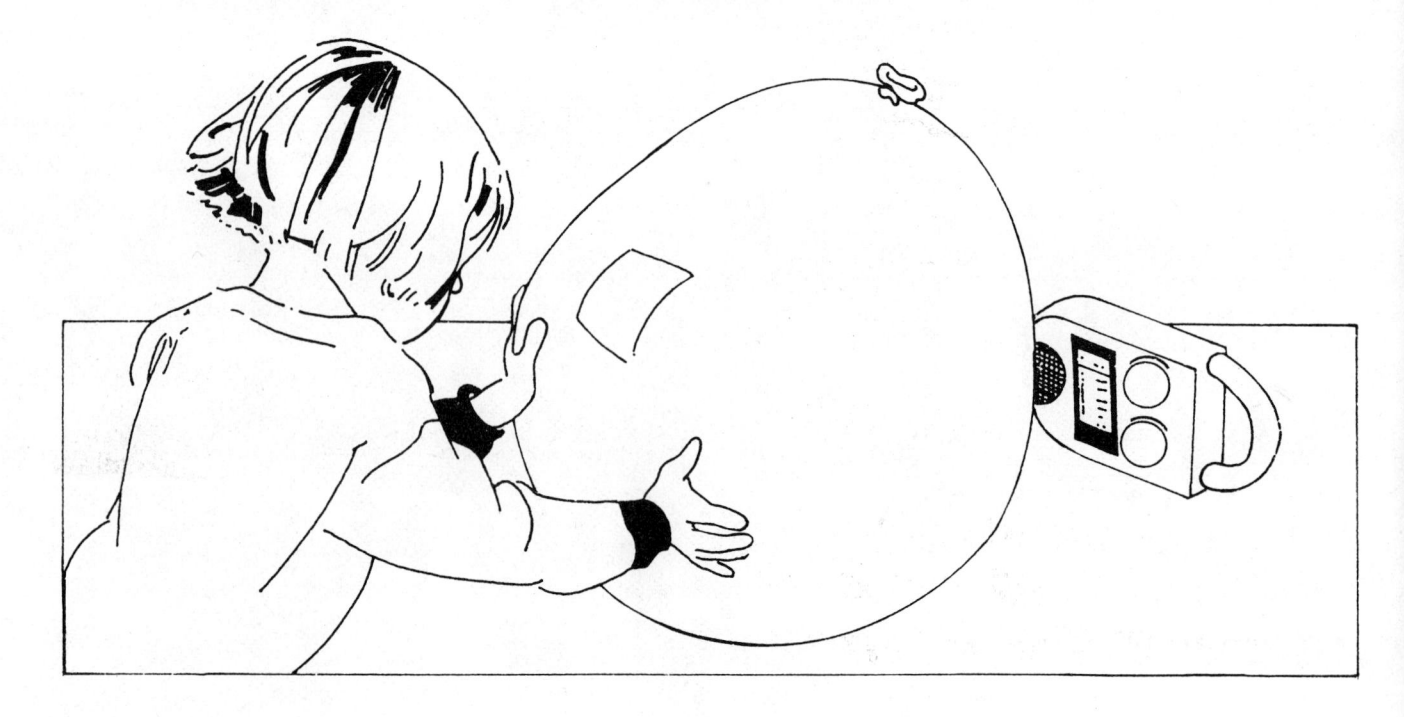

▲ Name _____

Can you hear through wood?

You will need: a friend to work with; a table; a coin.

▲ Stand at one end of the table.
▲ Ask your friend to use a coin to tap on the other end of the table. Can you hear the soft sound?

▲ Now put your ear against the table.

▲ Ask your friend to tap again. Can you hear the sound? Is it louder or softer?
▲ Can you hear through metal?

▲ ESSENTIALS FOR SCIENCE: Sound

▲ Name _____

Can sounds go along string?

You will need: a piece of string; two metal spoons.

▲ Tie your spoons in the middle of the string.
▲ Hold the ends of the string to your ears.
▲ Shake the string.

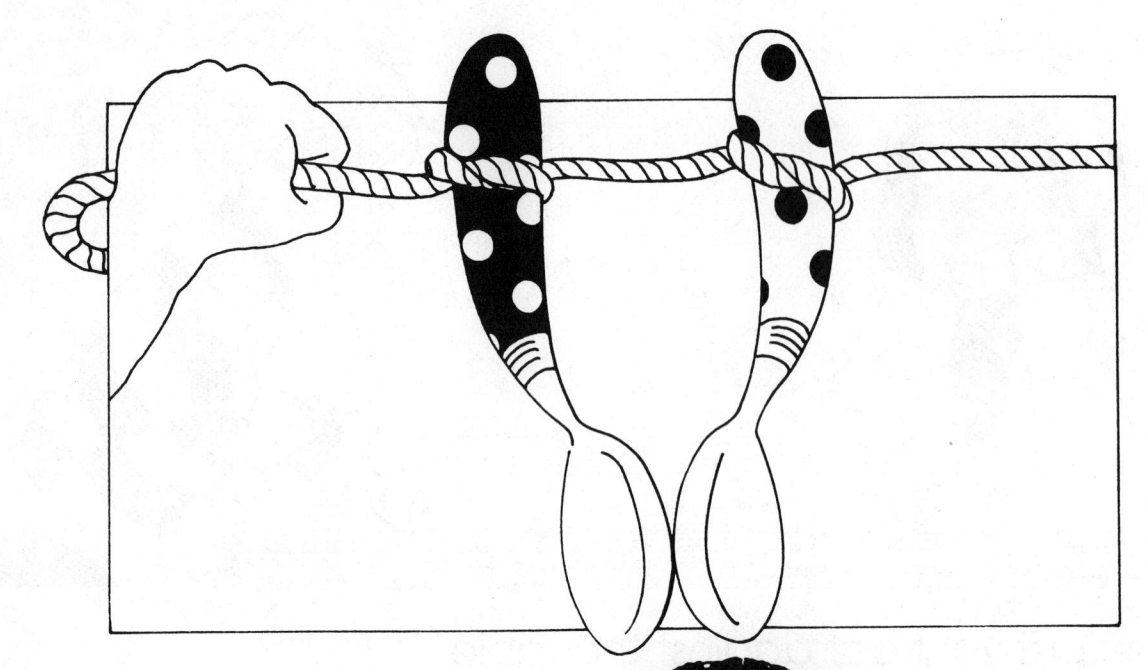

▲ Can you hear the spoons?
▲ Does sound go along string?
▲ What happens if you hang two pencils together?

▲ ESSENTIALS FOR SCIENCE: Sound

▲ Name _____

Make your own telephone

You will need: a friend to work with; two plastic pots; a long piece of thin string; two matchsticks.

▲ Ask an adult to make a hole in the bottom of each pot.

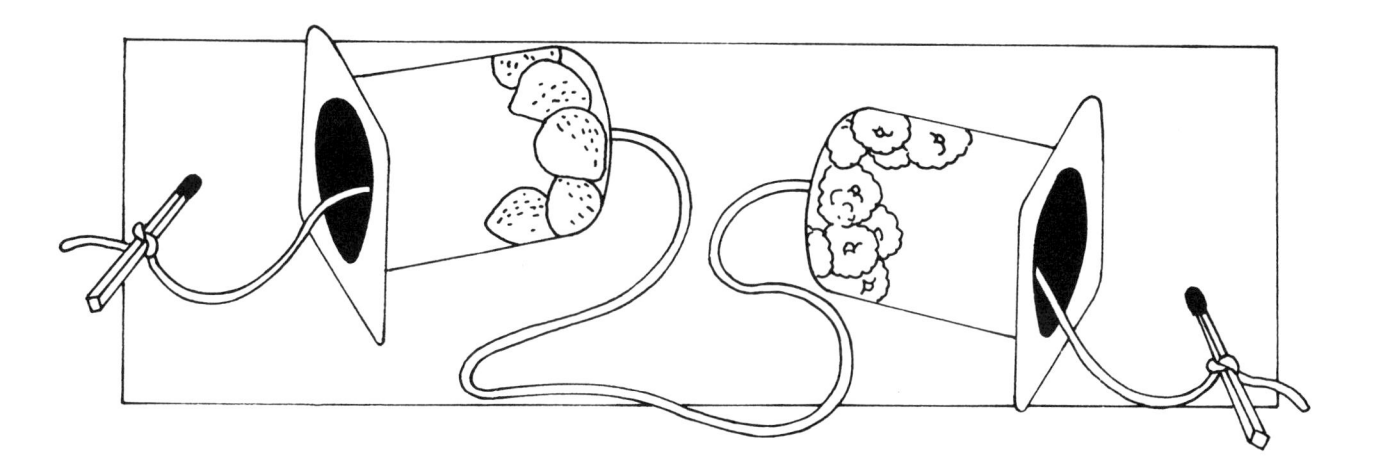

▲ Ask a friend to put one pot to his or her ear.
▲ Pull the string tight.
▲ Speak into your pot.

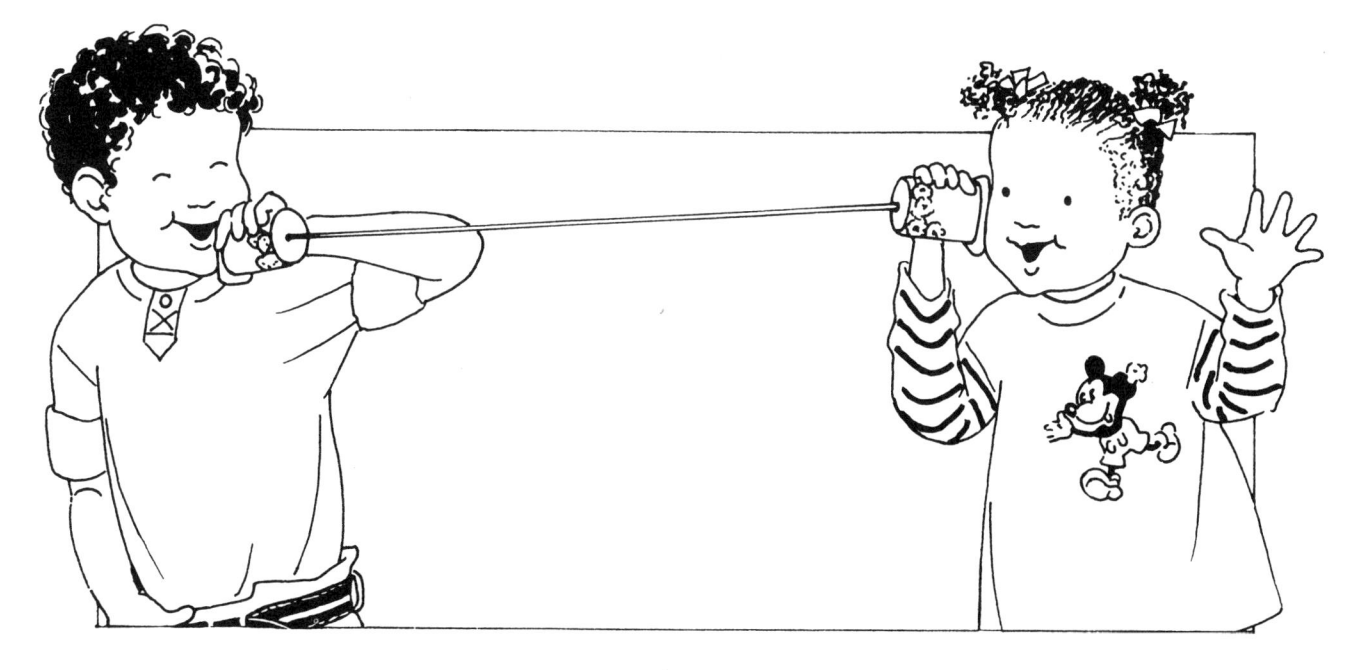

▲ Can your friend hear you?
▲ Can you make a telephone with three pots?

▲ ESSENTIALS FOR SCIENCE: Sound

▲ Name _____

Your voice

You make sounds with your voice. You talk. You shout. You sing. Something moves to make the sound.

▲ Put your hand here. Can you feel your voice moving?

▲ Do animals make sounds? What are they?
▲ Draw a picture of some animals and write what sounds they make.

▲ ESSENTIALS FOR SCIENCE: Sound

Name

Can you make your voice louder?

You will need: a friend to work with; a sheet of card; scissors; sticky tape.

▲ Roll your card like this.

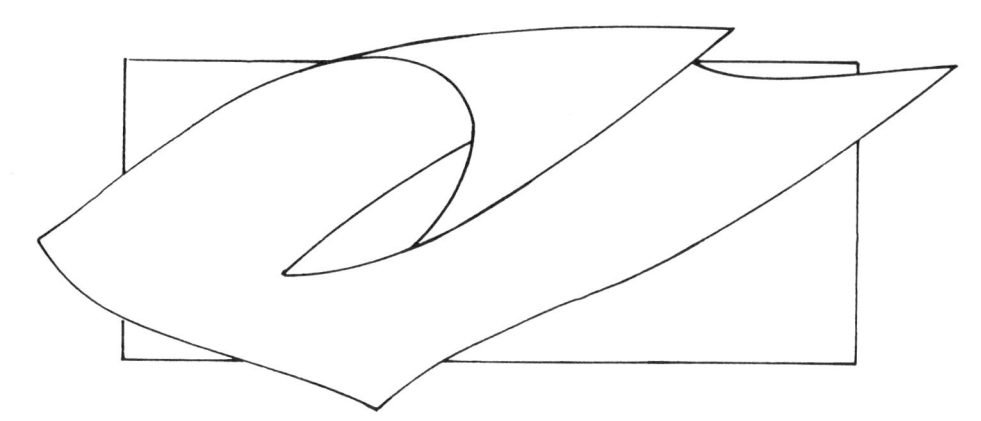

▲ Fix it in place with tape.

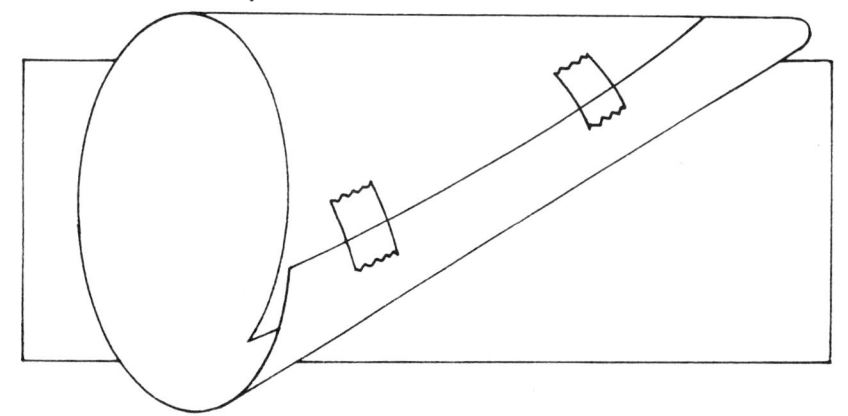

▲ Speak to your friend with the megaphone.
▲ Speak to your friend without the megaphone.

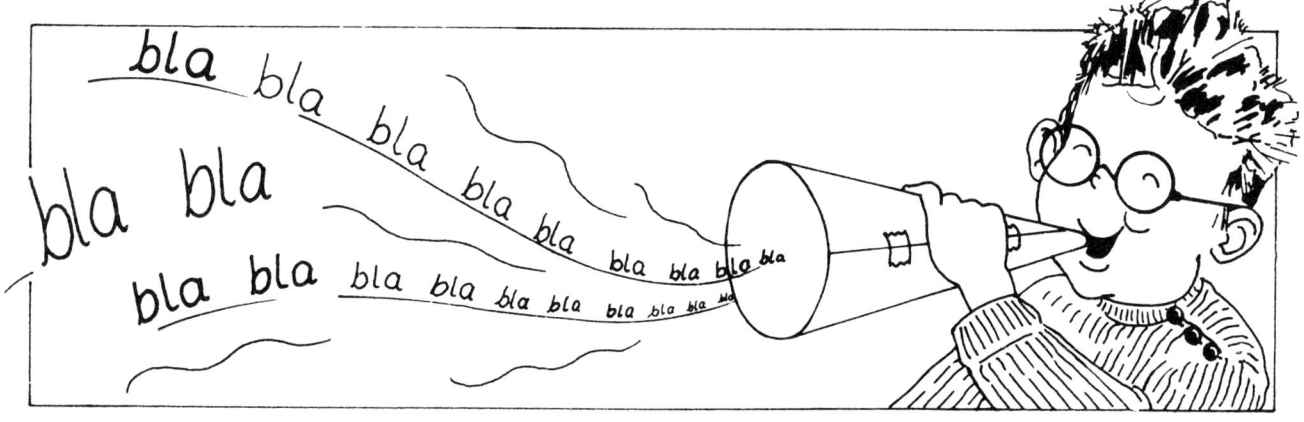

▲ Ask your friend which sounds loudest.
▲ Make large and small megaphones. Which one works best?

▲ ESSENTIALS FOR SCIENCE: Sound

▲ Name _____

Musical instruments

▲ Look at these musical instruments.
▲ How could you get a sound from each one?
▲ Draw a line to each to show how it is played.

blow   pluck   bang

ESSENTIALS FOR SCIENCE: Sound

▲ Name _____

Make a drum

You will need: a plastic basin or margarine tub; a thin plastic bag; sticky tape; scissors; a knitting needle; a few grains of rice; sugar.

▲ Cut a piece out of the plastic bag.
▲ Fix it to the container like this.

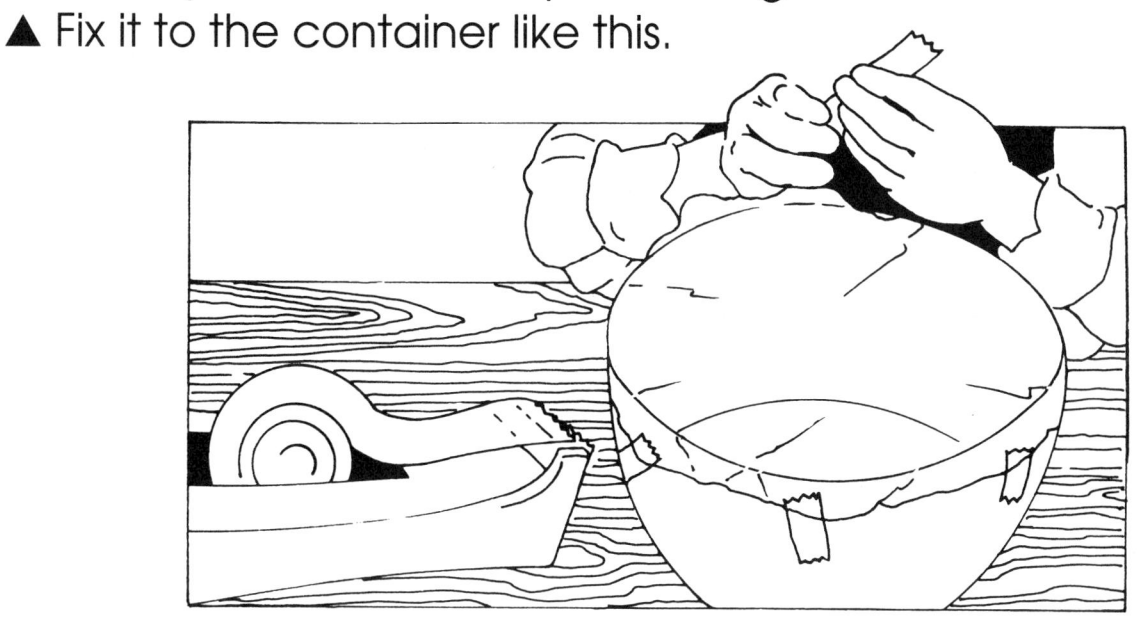

▲ Put a few grains of rice on your drum.
▲ Tap your drum with the knitting needle.

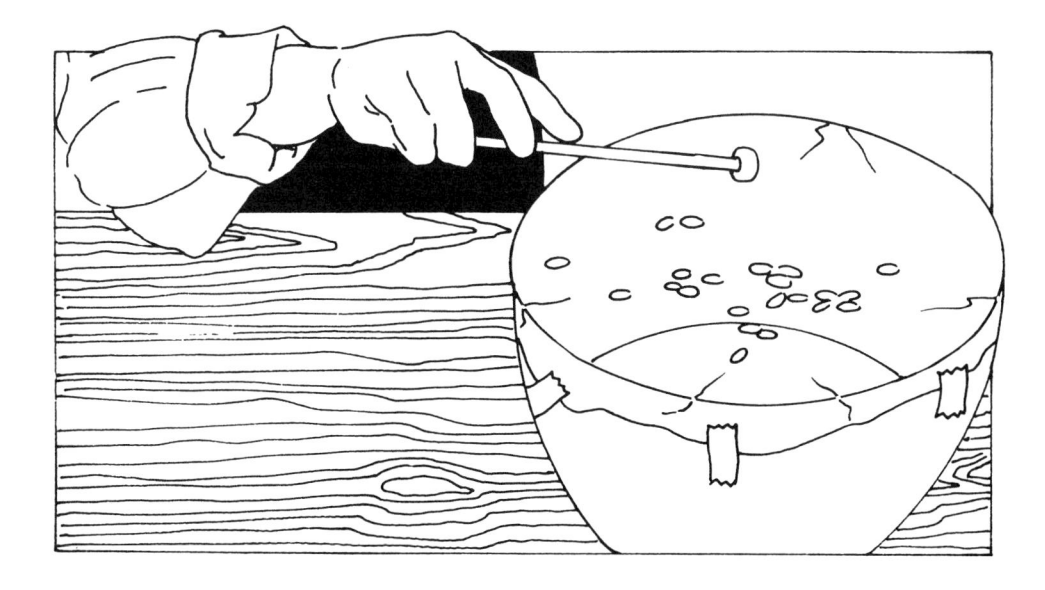

▲ What does the rice do?
▲ Will grains of sugar do the same thing?

▲ ESSENTIALS FOR SCIENCE: Sound

▲ Name _____

Make some maracas

You will need: two plastic pots; a clean plastic bottle; a short round stick; dried peas or rice; sticky tape or glue.

This man is playing maracas.

▲ Make your own maracas.
▲ Put peas or rice in one pot. Join the other pot to it.

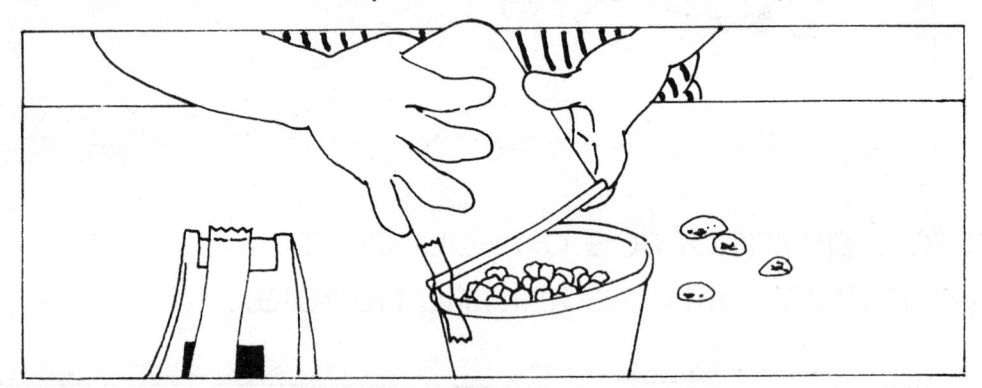

▲ Shake your maracas. How many different sounds can you make?
▲ Make different kinds of maracas.

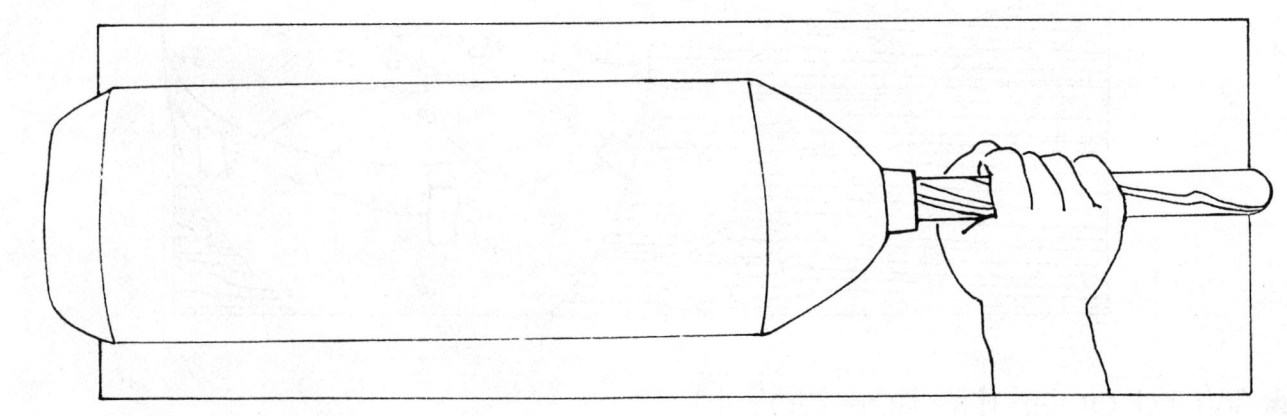

▲ Do they make different sounds?

▲ ESSENTIALS FOR SCIENCE: Sound

▲ Name _____

Make a guitar

You will need: a plastic box; eight rubber bands (some long, some short, some thick, some thin); ballpoint pens.

▲ Put the rubber bands round the box.
▲ Pluck them. Do they all make the same sound?

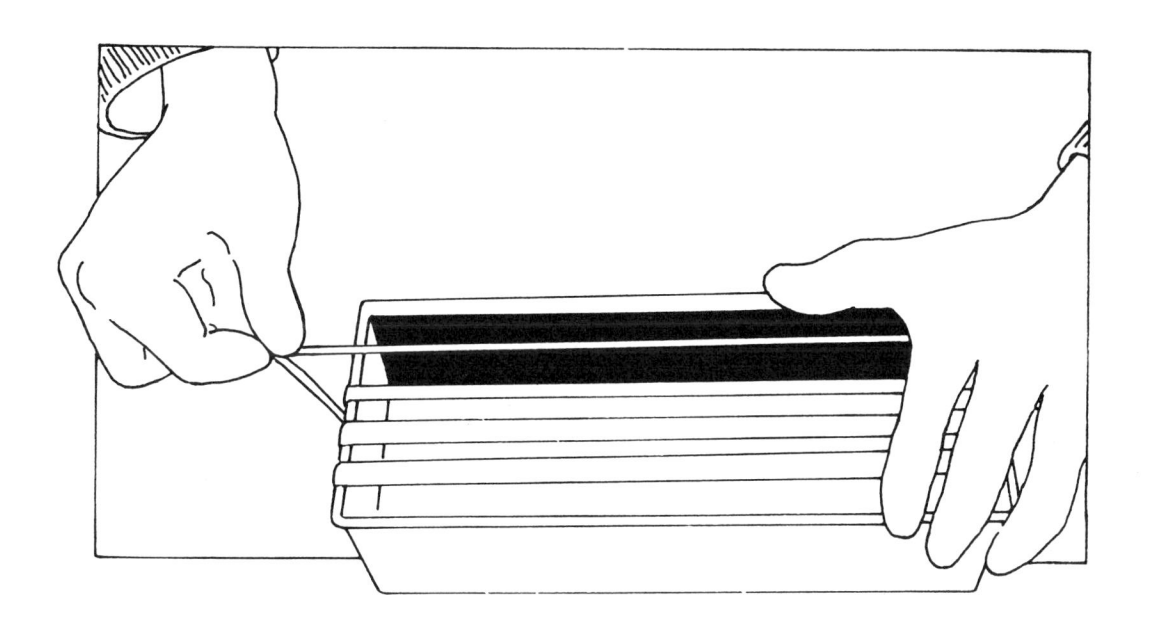

▲ Pull the rubber bands tight by putting ballpoint pens under them. Do they still make the same sound?

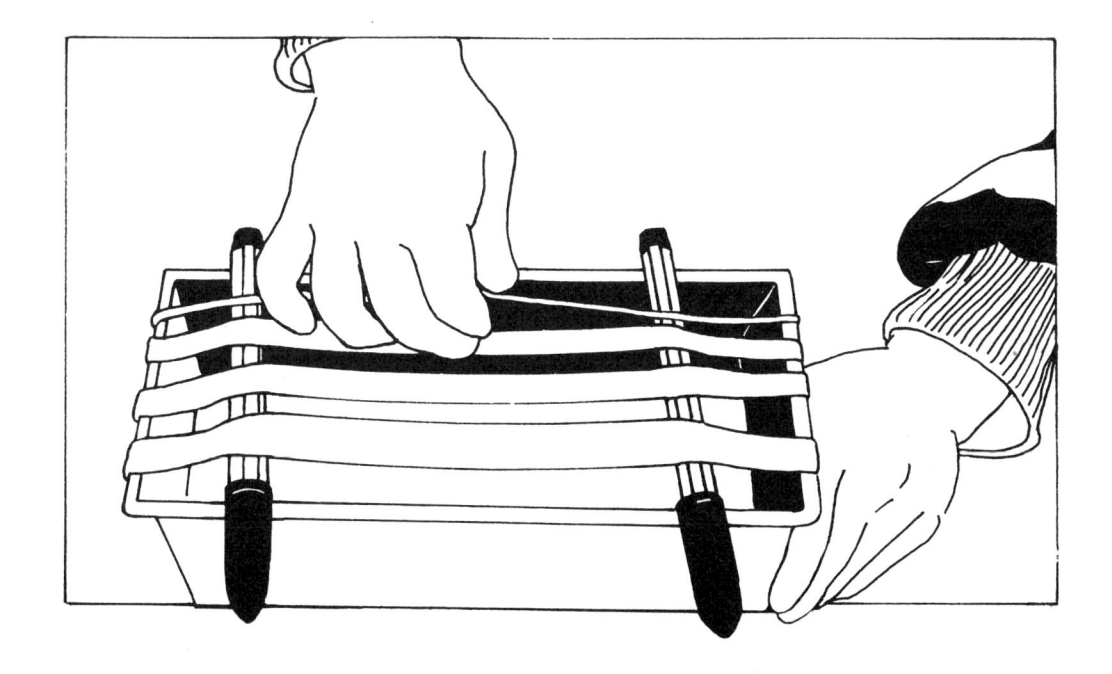

ESSENTIALS FOR SCIENCE: Sound

▲ Name _____

Bottle sounds

⚠

You will need: bottles of different shapes and sizes.

▲ Blow across the top of each bottle. What do you hear?
▲ Do all the bottles sound the same?

▲ Does it matter what the bottles are made from?

▲ ESSENTIALS FOR SCIENCE: Sound

▲ Name _____

Musical bottles ⚠️

You will need: glass bottles; water; a metal spoon; a plastic spoon; a wooden spoon.

▲ Pour different amounts of water in each bottle.
▲ Blow across each bottle. What do you hear?

▲ Tap each bottle. What do you hear?

▲ Does a plastic spoon make the same sound?
▲ Does a wooden spoon make the same sound?

▲ ESSENTIALS FOR SCIENCE: Sound

▲ Name _____

Sounds can bounce

You will need: a friend to work with; two bricks or blocks of wood; two cardboard tubes; sticky tape; a watch that ticks; a plate.

▲ Fix the tubes like this.

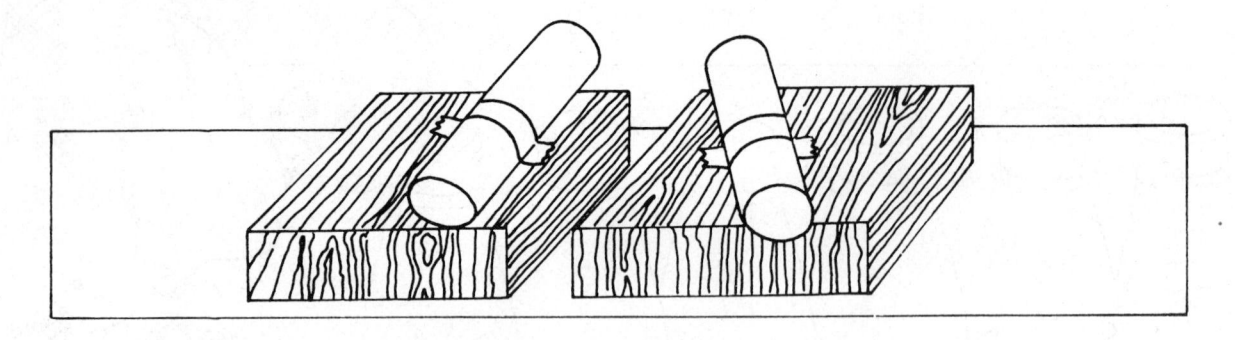

▲ Put the watch just inside one tube. Can you hear it ticking?

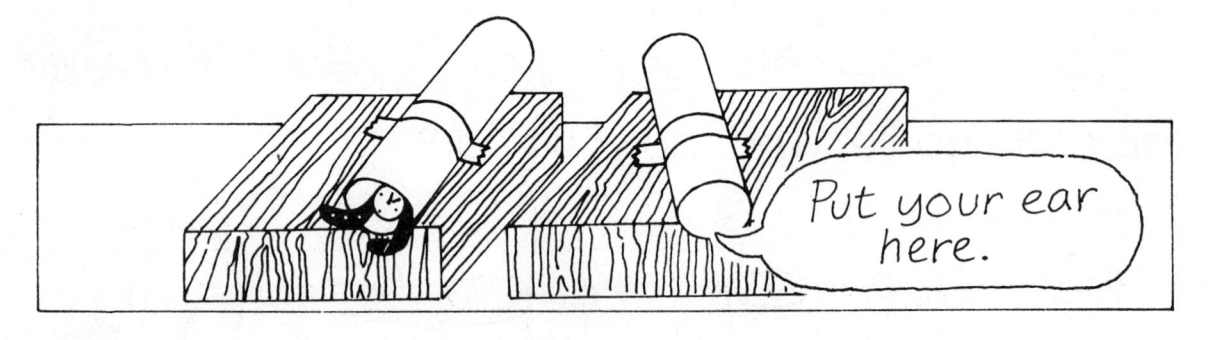

Put your ear here.

▲ Ask your friend to hold a plate near the tubes. Can you hear the watch ticking now?

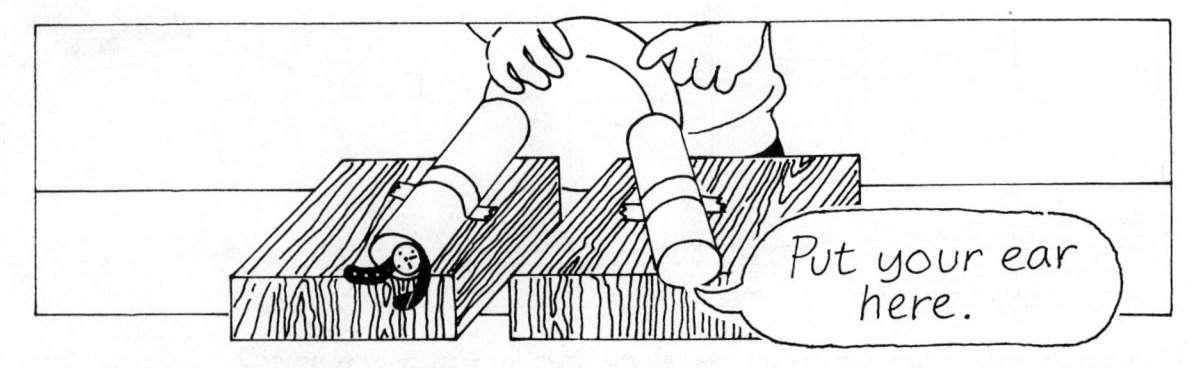

Put your ear here.

▲ What happens to the sound of the watch?
▲ Try other things instead of the plate. Which works best?

▲ ESSENTIALS FOR SCIENCE: Sound

▲ Name _____

Making echoes

You will need: a large bucket.

▲ Hold the bucket like this.

▲ Shout into it. What do you hear?
▲ Where else can you hear echoes? Draw some here.

▲ ESSENTIALS FOR SCIENCE: Sound

▲ Name _____

Sound messages

Sounds can give us messages.
Bells, sirens and whistles can do this.
Here are some message sounds.

▲ Look at each one.
Is it a bell, a siren or a whistle?

▲ Think of some more.

▲ ESSENTIALS FOR SCIENCE: Sound

▲ Name _____

Noise

You will need: a small radio (or a ticking clock); a box with a lid; newspaper.

We call sounds we don't like noise. How can we stop noise?
▲ Turn the radio on.
▲ Put your hands over your ears. Can you still hear the radio?

▲ Put the radio in a box. Can you hear it?

▲ Pack newspaper around the radio. Can you still hear it?

▲ What other materials will stop noise?

▲ Name _____

Match the sounds

▲ Match these sounds. Draw a line to the right picture.

Buzz!

Moo!

Woof!

Boo hoo!

clip-clop

miaow!

▲ ESSENTIALS FOR SCIENCE: Sound

Contents

Teachers' notes	1
Finding out about paper	5
The feel of paper	6
Which material is paper?	7
Paper we use in school	8
Paper at the post office	9
Packaging with paper	10
Paper for mopping up spills	11
Paper we throw away	12
Making your own paper	13
Papier mâché	14
How strong is paper?	15
Drops of water on paper	16
How well does paper wear?	17
Which paper can you see through?	18
A collection of fabrics	19
Fabrics at home	20
What are you wearing today?	21
Fabric, thread and fibre	22
Types of fabric	23
How strong are threads?	24
Weaving	25
Keeping warm and keeping cool	26
Which fabric keeps you warm?	27
Wet fabric and dry fabric	28
Drying fabric	29
Which fabric for a waterproof hat?	30
Which fabrics are hard wearing?	31
Litter: paper and fabrics	32

Teachers' notes

Aims of this book

The aims of this book are:
- to encourage children to use their senses to describe the properties of materials such as texture, shape, colour and weight;
- to encourage children to look for similarities and differences in the materials and to find ways of grouping them;
- to raise awareness of the variety of ways in which we use papers and fabrics;
- to introduce the idea of natural and manufactured materials;
- to show what is meant by a fibre and a fabric;
- to show what is meant by 'real' paper;
- to demonstrate ways of making paper and fabric;
- to show the effect of light and water on materials;
- to raise awareness of recycling materials;
- to examine some of the properties of materials.

Scientific background

This information will help you to understand the scientific concepts and ideas covered in this book. It goes beyond the level of understanding expected of most children but will give you the confidence to ask and answer questions and to guide the children in their investigations.

Materials

Materials are the substances from which things are or can be made. This includes the use of the word 'material' to describe fabric or cloth.

Natural materials such as cotton, wool, silk and wood come from plants and animals.

Manufactured or synthetic materials are made from other natural materials such as petroleum chemicals or coal to produce for example, rayon, nylon, polyester and acrylic fabrics. Wood is a major component in the manufacture of paper.

When undertaking this topic, a wide range of papers and fabrics should be available for the children to handle and investigate.

Fibres

A fibre is a long thin strand of material. Threads are made from fibres which have been spun together. Fabric is material made from woven or tangled threads.

Cotton, silk and animal hair are natural fibres. Cotton comes from the fibres which encase the cotton seeds in the 'cotton pod'. Denim, calico and poplin are cotton fabrics. Silk threads come from the woven cocoon of the silkworm caterpillar. Animal hair such as sheep's wool or camel hair are woven into cloth. Woollen garments may be labelled as tweed.

Manufactured fibres are labelled in a confusing number of trade names but children can examine a variety of synthetic fibres such as those made from nylon, polyester and acrylic. Manufactured fibres tend to be more hard wearing than natural fibres.

Many fabrics contain a mixture of natural and manufactured fibres such as cotton/polyester and wool/nylon mixtures.

▲ ESSENTIALS FOR SCIENCE: Paper and fabrics

Paper

Most paper is made from softwoods such as pine and spruce but paper can be made from cotton, linen and the leaves of Esparto grass. Recycled paper can be made from newspapers and rags.

The wood is chopped into small pieces and boiled in chemicals to produce a pulpy liquid which is bleached and spread over a moving mesh. The water drains away leaving a thin layer of pulp. The fibres in the wood pulp become enmeshed forming a 'felt'. Further water is squeezed out of the paper as it is pressed and dried between large rollers to finish with a continuous roll of smooth paper.

Notes on individual activities

Page 5: Finding out about paper

Key idea: to find out similarities and differences between papers.
Extension: devise other tests to carry out, for example cutting, painting on and soaking paper.
Safety precaution: use a water-based glue.

Page 6: The feel of paper

Key idea: some papers are smoother than others. Smooth paper is made from fibres which are finer than those used for rougher paper.
Developing the investigation: suggest that the children find other ways of grading the papers.
Extension: press a piece of sticky tape on to each type of paper then pull it off. What is on it?
Safety precaution: use a water-based glue.

Page 7: Which material is paper?

Key ideas: real paper is made from fibres pressed together. Real paper tears.
Developing the investigation: explain that 'real' paper is made of a mat of fibres. Devise more tests to find out how real paper and others are used. Which are the best for painting on? What are the 'other papers' made from?
Extension: let the children find out how paper is made and perhaps make some themselves.

Page 8: Paper we use in school

Key ideas: there are many different kinds of paper and card which are used in different ways.
Developing the investigation: encourage the children to relate the properties of the paper to usage. Suggest that they find their own ways of sorting the paper.

Page 9: Paper at the post office

Key ideas: there are many different kinds of paper. Paper has many uses.
Developing the investigation: make a collection of the different types of paper at a post office. Look for watermarks in banknotes and discuss them.

Page 10: Packaging with paper

Key idea: different kinds of paper and card are used to package a variety of goods.
Developing the investigation: make a collection of wrappings and sort these in a variety of ways; for example cartons which have a waterproof coating, packaging material and so on.
Extension: find ways of packing pieces of chalk in a box so that the chalk will not break when the box is rattled or dropped.

Page 11: Paper for mopping up spills

Key idea: certain papers absorb water.
Developing the investigation: discuss different ways to mop up spills. Discuss the word 'absorb'. Encourage the children to describe the papers before they test them and to predict which will absorb the most water.
Extension: mop up different substances such as tomato ketchup, jam or washing up liquid. Which paper towels are best for these? Do the papers work better when they are damp?

Page 12: Paper we throw away

Key ideas: we throw away large amounts of paper and card. Some of this can be recycled.
Developing the investigation: discuss the kinds of paper and card which are thrown away at school. Explain that many kinds of paper can be recycled. This saves water and trees.

Page 13: Making your own paper

Key idea: used paper can be recycled to make new paper.
Developing the investigation: the children need to use paper which will absorb water and form a pulp. Place the damp paper between layers of cotton material and press or iron it to make a thinner piece of paper. Experiment with food colourings and natural dyes to colour the paper.

Page 14: Make a papier mâché head

Key ideas: used paper can be recycled. Using paper for papier mâché modelling changes the properties of the original paper.
Extension: how has the paper changed when used in this way? Is it stronger when it is wet or dry? Is it easy to tear? Is it flexible?
Safety precautions: do not use wallpaper paste containing a fungicide. Make sure that children wash their hands after handling the paste.

Page 15: How strong is paper?

Key idea: different types of paper under tension have different strengths.
Developing the investigation: encourage the

▲ ESSENTIALS FOR SCIENCE: Paper and fabrics

children to make their tests fair by treating each paper in the same way. Examine the tears with a hand lens to find out more about the differences between the papers. The weights can be standard or non-standard. Try the test on different carrier bags and other fabrics.
Safety precaution: ensure that the hook is fixed low down on the wall and that the children keep their feet well clear when adding the weights.

Page 16: Drops of water on paper

Key idea: papers vary in their ability to absorb water.
Developing the investigation: predict how the drops of water will behave on the paper. Add food colouring to the water to make it easier to see what happens.
Extension: observe how the water spreads over the paper. Does it spread more in one direction than another? What does this say about the fibre patterns? Tear the paper both ways and use a hand lens to look at the fibres. Are there more fibres going in one direction than the other?
Safety precaution: use a water-based glue.

Page 17: How well does paper wear?

Key idea: some papers wear better than others.
Developing the investigation: discuss times when paper needs to wear well.

Page 18: Which paper can you see through?

Key ideas: some types of paper are transparent, some are opaque and some are translucent.
Developing the investigation: discuss the words transparent, opaque and translucent.
Extension: make a simple black outline drawing and test the translucent paper by placing each piece over the drawing.

Page 19: A collection of fabrics

Key idea: to encourage children to describe a fabric using their senses.
Developing the investigation: provide a variety of fabrics such as carpet pieces, cloths, curtain and upholstery fabrics. Encourage the children to devise their own simple tests. Let them tell others what they have found out.
Safety precaution: use a water-based glue.

Page 20: Fabrics at home

Key idea: fabrics have many uses.
Developing the investigation: let the children find different fabrics used in school. Discuss and colour the picture on the sheet. They can do the same for their bedroom.

Page 21: What are you wearing today?

Key idea: garments are made from fibres which are natural, manufactured or a mixture of the two.

Developing the investigation: discuss the different kinds of natural fibres used in fabrics. Explain that other fibres are made by machines from chemicals. Clothes are often made from a mixture of natural and manufactured fibres. Make a graph to show which garments are mostly made from synthetic fibres or a mixture.

Page 22: Fabric, thread and fibre

Key idea: to see how a fabric is made.
Developing the investigation: look at the fabric to see how it is woven together. Find words to describe the colour, texture and smell of the fabric. The children will see that a thread is made from fibres which are spun together. Compare coarse fabric with other fabrics such as cotton or nylon.
Safety precaution: use a water-based glue.

Page 23: Types of fabrics

Key idea: fabrics are made from fibres which are interlaced together.
Developing the investigation: felt and J-cloths are tangled fibres; T-shirts, socks and jumpers are knitted fibres, and shirts, trousers and skirts are usually woven. Using clean garments, investigate the examples and make comparisons between the different kinds of fabrics. Make labels and sort the examples into sets.
Extension: compare fabrics with other materials such as leather or rubber.
Safety precaution: use a water-based glue.

Page 24: How strong are threads?

Key idea: some threads are stronger than others.
Likely outcome: the natural threads are probably not as strong as the manufactured ones. The children may not be able to break some of the threads.
Developing the investigation: put a cushion or mat underneath the bucket and hook it so that it is near the ground and does not have far to fall. Look at the way the thread has broken. Do all the threads break in the same place? What do the broken ends look like?
Extension: provide a collection of ropes, strings and knitting yarns. Make observations about them and look at the different kinds of fibres with a hand lens. What are the threads used for?
Safety precaution: ensure that the hook is fixed low down on the wall and that the children keep their feet well clear when adding the weights.

Page 25: Weaving

Key idea: threads can be woven to make fabric.
Developing the investigation: provide examples of coarse woven fabrics to show the under-over pattern of the weave. Let the children find the threads which go up and down (the warp

threads) and those which go from side to side (the weft threads).

Page 26: Keeping warm and keeping cool
Key idea: we wear different clothes to suit the seasonal weather conditions.
Developing the investigation: make a display of clothes worn in summer and winter. Do the fabrics feel warm or cool? Are they knitted or woven? Is one side the same as the other? Is there a lining? Is it stretchy? Make comparisons.
Extension: find out about clothes to sleep in, for dressing up, for sport.

Page 27: Which fabric keeps you warm?
Key idea: some fabrics are good insulators.
Likely outcome: the woollen fabric will keep the can the warmest. The uncovered can will be coolest.
Developing the investigation: discuss the ways we keep warm in winter and the kinds of clothes we wear. Display some winter clothes and examine the kinds of fabric which keep us warm.
Safety precaution: use hot, not boiling, water.

Page 28: Wet fabric and dry fabric
Key ideas: there are differences between wet and dry fabrics. Hot water changes some fabrics.
Developing the investigation: discuss how fabrics change when wet. Make observations about the dry fabric such as colour, texture, thickness and weave. How many differences can the children find when the fabric is wet?
Safety precaution: use hot, not boiling, water.

Page 29: Drying fabric
Key ideas: certain conditions cause fabrics to dry more quickly than others.
Developing the investigation: compare different drying places and the way different fabrics dry.
Extension: hang the fabric in different ways – stretched out, hung by one peg or folded. Does this make a difference to the drying time?

Page 30: Which fabric for a waterproof hat?
Key idea: some fabrics do not let water through.
Developing the investigation: examine and describe the fabrics. Treat each fabric in the same way to make it a fair test.
Extension: which fabric absorbed the most water? These are the fabrics on which water spreads out. Find ways to make a fabric waterproof, for example, by rubbing the surface with a candle or crayon. Let the children test the waxed fabric.

Page 31: Which fabrics are hard wearing?
Key idea: some fabrics wear better than others.
Developing the investigation: predict which fabrics will be hard wearing. Describe what happens during the test. Try tearing the fabric or rubbing it over a rough surface such as a brick.
Extension: which parts of clothes wear out? Why?
Safety precaution: use a water-based glue.

Page 32: Litter: paper and fabrics
Key idea: most litter made from paper or fabric shows changes when left outside for a time.
Developing the investigation: go on a litter hunt to look for signs of decay in litter. Compare the similarities and differences between the two collections after a fortnight. The outside collection could be left outside for longer to see what happens.
Extension: bury a third collection a few centimetres below ground. What happens to litter when it is underground?
Safety precaution: do not let children handle litter without wearing polythene gloves.

National Curriculum: Science

In addition to the PoS for AT1, the following PoS are relevant to this book.

- Pupils should collect and find similarities and differences between a variety of everyday materials. These should include natural and manufactured materials. They should explore the properties of these materials referring, for example, to their shape, colour and texture, and consider some of their everyday uses. They should know how some can be changed by simple processes such as... squashing, bending and twisting.

- Pupils should develop an awareness of which materials they are using are naturally occurring and which are manufactured. They should explore the effects of heating some everyday substances... in order to understand how heating and cooling bring about melting and solidifying. They should observe materials... which change permanently on heating.

Scottish 5 – 14 Curriculum

Environmental studies
Attainment outcomes: Science in the environment (materials)
Living with technology (effects of technology)
Investigating (finding out; recording; interpreting; reporting)

▲ ESSENTIALS FOR SCIENCE: Paper and fabrics

▲ Name _____

Finding out about paper

You will need: different types of paper (all the same size); a hand lens; glue.

▲ Find out how the papers are different. How are they the same?

▲ Complete the chart below.

Paper sample (stick a piece here)				
Can you write on it?				
Does it crumple easily?				
Does it tear easily?				
Is the paper shiny?				
Does it make a noise when shaken?				
What is it used for?				
Can you trace it?				

▲ ESSENTIALS FOR SCIENCE: Paper and fabrics

▲ Name _____

The feel of paper

You will need: five different kinds of paper, such as writing, blotting, mounting, kitchen roll, paper towel or glossy paper; a hand lens; glue.

▲ Do all the papers feel the same? Do they feel the same on both sides?

▲ Grade the papers from the roughest to the smoothest. Cut out examples of the paper to stick on the grid below.

Roughest ⟵⟶ Smoothest

▲ How is the roughest paper different from the smoothest paper?

▲ Tear the papers. Look at the fibres along the tear. Do smooth papers have different kinds of fibres from rough papers?

▲ ESSENTIALS FOR SCIENCE: Paper and fabrics

▲ Name _____

Which material is paper?

You will need: newspapers; tissue paper; writing paper; paper towels; aluminium foil; plastic; polythene; cellophane; greaseproof paper; thin cardboard; food wrap; hand lens; a pencil.

Real paper is made from fibres which are pressed together. A fibre is a long, thin thread of material like a hair.

▲ Dampen and tear the papers.

▲ Use a hand lens to look at the tear. Can you see any fibres? The ones with fibres are real paper.

▲ Make two sets.

paper with fibre

other paper

▲ What are the differences between the two sets?

▲ ESSENTIALS FOR SCIENCE: Paper and fabrics

▲ Name _____

Paper we use in school

You will need: a variety of paper and objects made from paper and card from around the school.

▲Look around your school. Make a collection of the different kinds of paper and card in use.

▲Sort the collection into sets according to how you use them.

▲Cut out the labels below and use them to help you sort the paper. Make extra labels for your own ideas.

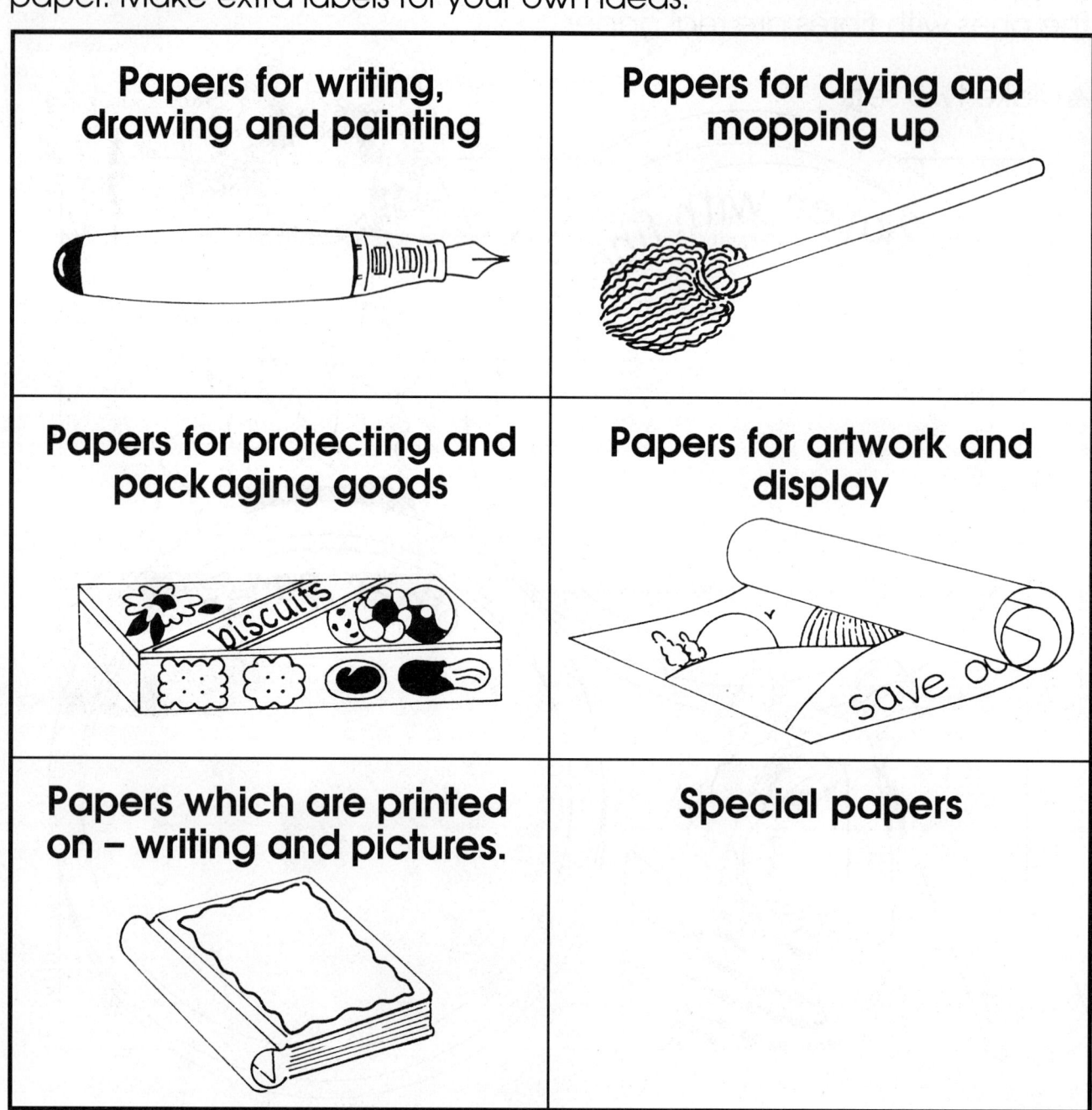

Papers for writing, drawing and painting	Papers for drying and mopping up
Papers for protecting and packaging goods	Papers for artwork and display
Papers which are printed on – writing and pictures.	Special papers

▲Are some papers in more than one set?

▲ ESSENTIALS FOR SCIENCE: Paper and fabrics

▲ Name _____

Paper at the post office

▲ Tick everything in the picture which is made from paper or card.

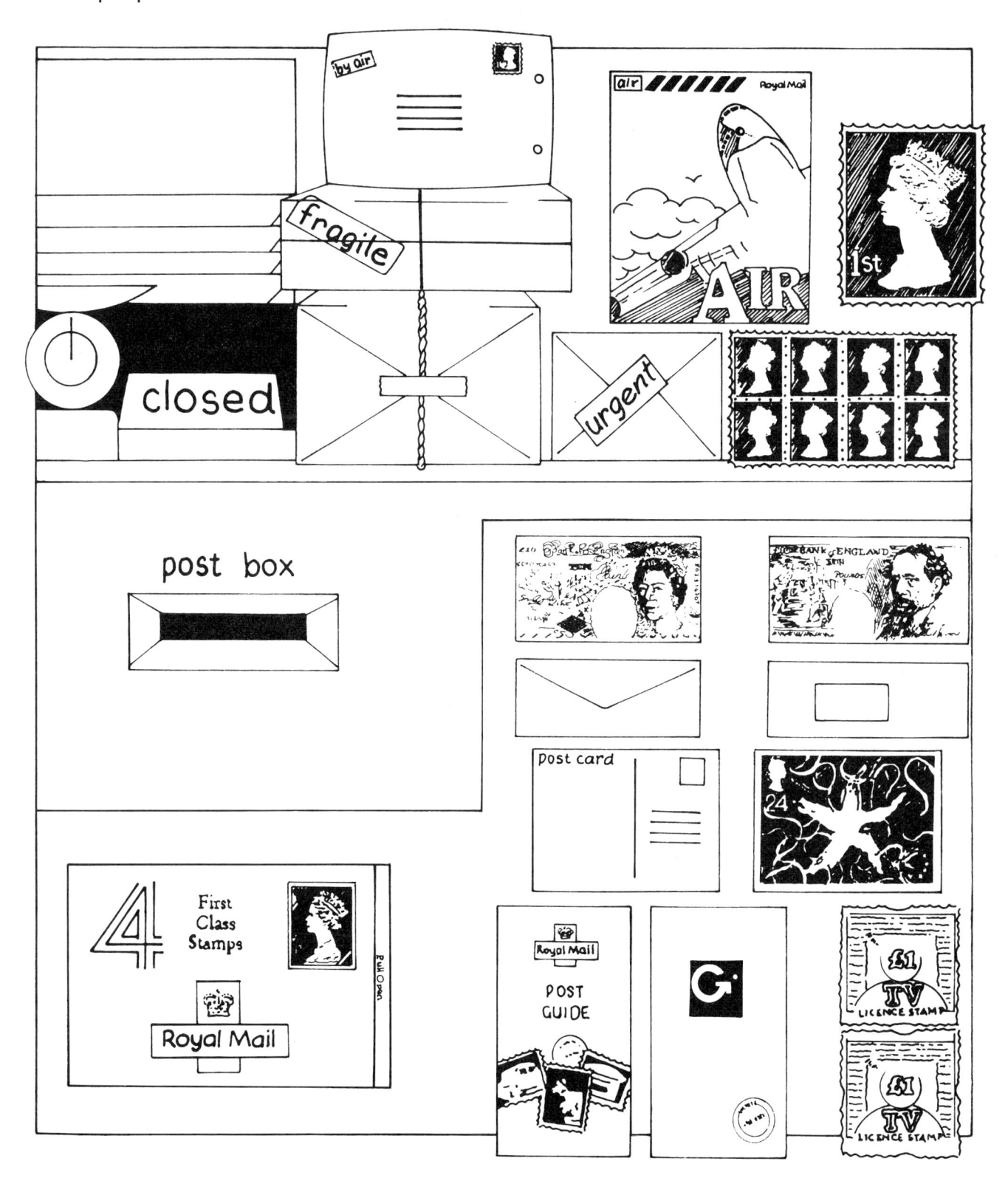

▲ Make a collection of the different sorts of paper found in a post office.

▲ ESSENTIALS FOR SCIENCE: Paper and fabrics

▲ Name _____

Packaging with paper

You will need: a pencil.

▲ Look out for the goods we buy which are packaged in paper or card.

▲ Draw a circle round all the goods in the picture below which are packaged in paper or card.

▲ Add your own ideas on the back of this sheet.

▲ Make a collection of paper and card packaging. Find ways of sorting them.

▲ Name_____

Paper for mopping up spills

You will need: different kinds of paper used for mopping up spills, such as paper towels, tissues and kitchen roll; trays or plates; a magnifying glass; scissors; water.

▲ Cut all the paper to the same size.

▲ Use a magnifying glass to look closely at the paper.

▲ Which paper feels thick? Do any have more than one layer?

▲ Which do you think will mop up the most water?

▲ To find out, take a piece of paper and dip it in water. Shake the paper. Then squeeze out the water on to a tray. Do this with all types of paper. Which one soaked up the most water?

▲ Which is the best paper for mopping up spills?

▲ ESSENTIALS FOR SCIENCE: Paper and fabrics

▲ Name _____

Paper we throw away

Everyday we throw away different kinds of paper and card. Some of this could be used again to make new paper. This is called **recycling.**

▲Look at the picture below. Draw a ring round the kinds of waste paper and card which you find in your school.

▲List other types of waste paper which you find on the back of this sheet.

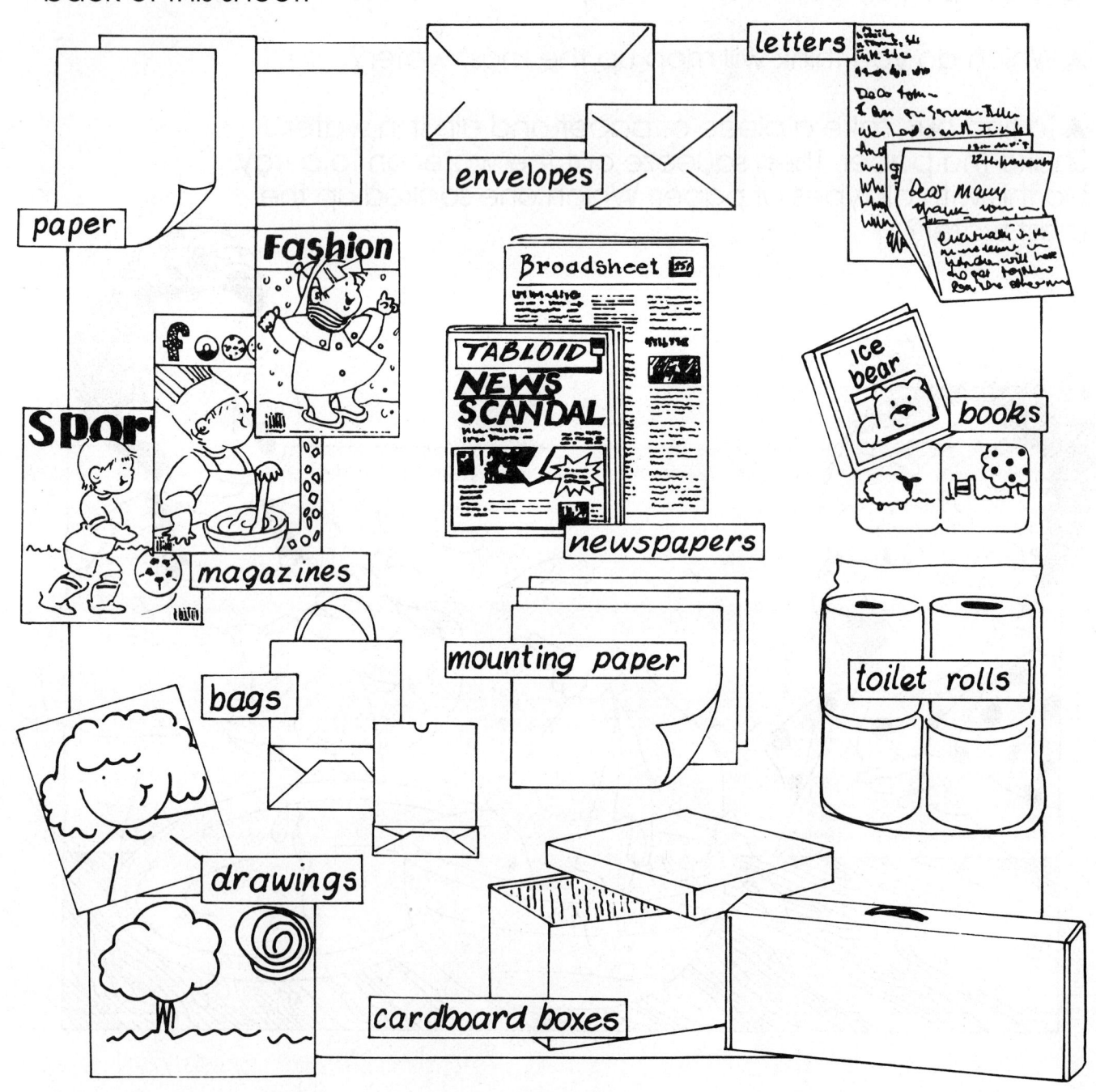

- letters
- envelopes
- paper
- magazines
- newspapers
- books
- mounting paper
- bags
- toilet rolls
- drawings
- cardboard boxes

▲What kinds of waste paper and card do you have at home?

▲ ESSENTIALS FOR SCIENCE: Paper and fabrics

▲ Name _____

Making your own paper

You will need: a net frame (called a deckle); water; tissue paper; a hand lens.

▲ Tear the paper into small pieces and soak them in water overnight.

▲ Mix the paper and water until it is a pulpy mixture that looks like porridge.

▲ Pour this on to the frame and spread it out evenly. Let this dry. You will have made a thick piece of paper.

▲ Look at your paper with a hand lens. Can you see the fibres?

▲ How could you make a thinner piece of paper?

▲ ESSENTIALS FOR SCIENCE: Paper and fabrics

▲ Name _____

Papier mâché ⚠

You will need: torn-up waste paper; flour and water paste or wallpaper paste (without fungicide); paint; wool.

▲Soak the torn-up waste paper in the paste. This is papier mâché.

▲Use the papier mâché to make a model of the head of a person or animal.

▲Leave it to dry and then paint a face on it and stick on pieces of wool for hair.

▲How is the papier mâché different from the paper you used to make it from?

▲ ESSENTIALS FOR SCIENCE: Paper and fabrics   14

▲ Name _____

How strong is paper? ⚠

You will need: different kinds of paper, such as sugar paper, tissue paper, writing paper, greaseproof paper, brown parcel paper; weights; container to hold the weights; scissors; two bulldog clips; a hook fixed in a low position to the wall; a pencil.

▲ Cut out pieces of paper so that they are all the same size.

▲ Clip a bulldog clip to each end of the paper.

▲ Fix a container to one bulldog clip. Hang the other bulldog clip from a hook.

▲ Put the weights in the container one by one. Record how much weight the paper will hold before it tears.

▲ Which paper tears first? Which paper is the strongest?

▲ Is the strongest paper waterproof?

▲ ESSENTIALS FOR SCIENCE: Paper and fabrics

▲ Name _____

Drops of water on paper ⚠

You will need: a plastic dropper or drinking straw; a beaker; glue; a collection of different types of paper to test, such as drawing paper, sugar paper, writing paper, glossy paper, newspaper, waxed paper, greaseproof paper and wrapping paper.

▲ Place a piece of paper over the beaker.

▲ Use the dropper or straw to drop water on to the paper.

▲ Record what happens to the water on the chart below.

▲ Do the same with the other types of paper. Use the same number of drops of water each time.

Samples of paper	soaked through paper	Spread out	Stayed in a drop

▲ Sort the paper into sets by what happens.

▲ Do we have different uses for the different types of paper?

▲ ESSENTIALS FOR SCIENCE: Paper and fabrics

▲ Name _____

How well does paper wear?

You will need: a clipboard; sandpaper; different kinds of paper, such as greaseproof paper, tissue paper, brown parcel paper, waxed paper and writing paper.

▲ Examine the different kinds of paper. Describe them.

▲ Clip one piece of paper to the clipboard.

▲ Rub it with the sandpaper. Count the number of rubs or has a hole in it.

▲ Stick the paper on to a chart and write down the number of rubs.

▲ Which paper will wear best?

▲ ESSENTIALS FOR SCIENCE: Paper and fabrics

▲ Name _____

Which paper can you see through?

You will need: different types of paper, such as sugar paper, brown paper, tissue paper, crêpe paper, Cellophane, sweet papers, tracing paper and greaseproof paper; scissors; sticky tape.

▲Make a set of papers which you can see through. These are transparent.

▲Make a set of papers which you cannot see through. These are opaque.

▲Make a set of papers which you cannot see through clearly but which let some light through. These are translucent.

▲Choose one type of paper from each set and stick it behind these holes. Label which is which.

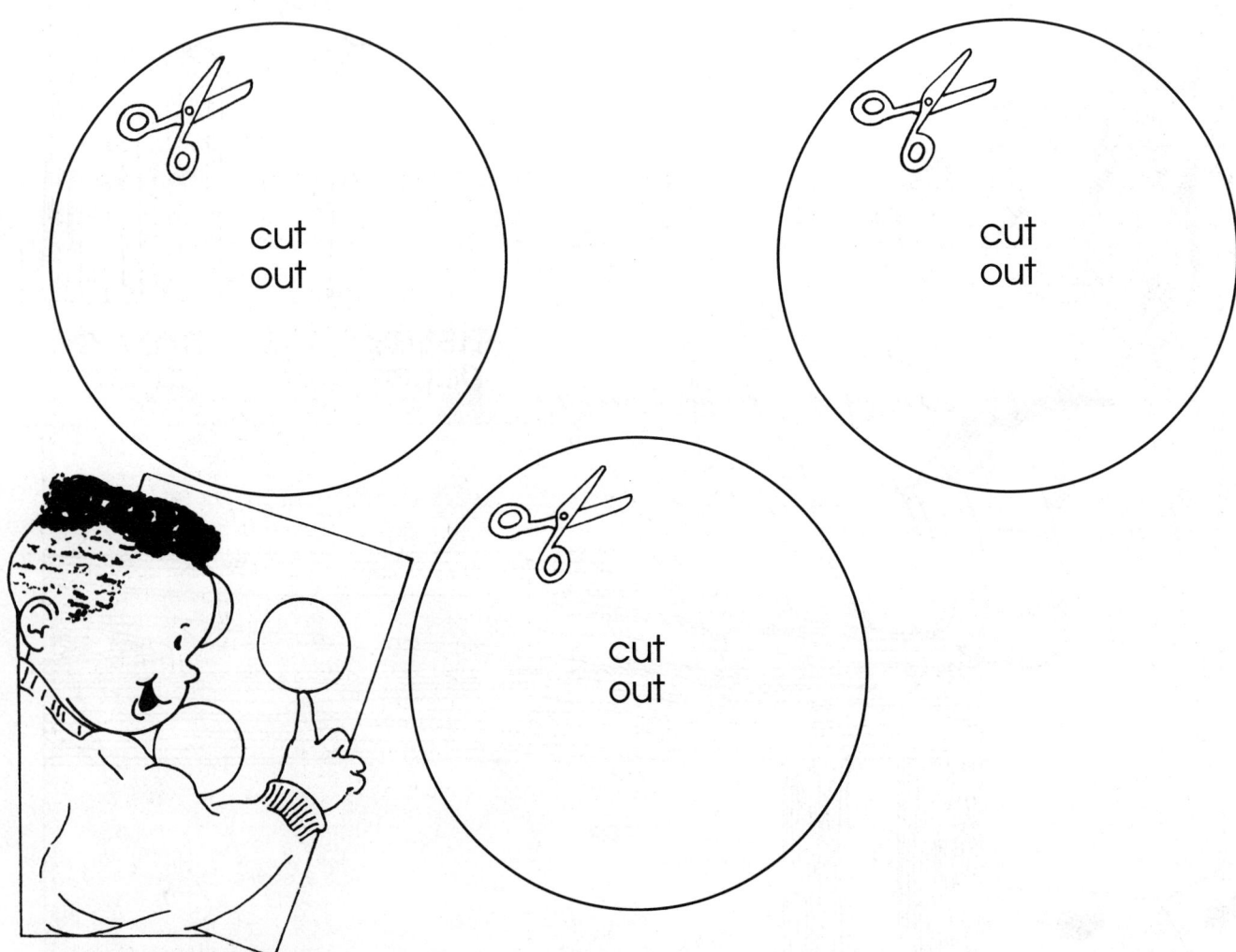

cut out

cut out

cut out

▲Which paper would you use to make a stained-glass window picture?

▲ ESSENTIALS FOR SCIENCE: Paper and fabrics

▲ Name _____

A collection of fabrics ⚠

You will need: a small piece of fabric; a hand lens; glue; a pencil.

▲Choose a fabric and look at it carefully.
What does it feel like? Is it thick or thin? What colour is it?
Has it a pattern? What is it made from? What do we use it for?

▲What else can you find out about it?

▲Stick your fabric in the space below and write down what you have found out about it.

stick fabric here

▲Look at what your friends have found out about their fabric.

▲ ESSENTIALS FOR SCIENCE: Paper and fabrics

▲ Name _____

Fabrics at home

▲ Look at the picture below and discuss it with your friends.

▲ Colour in all the things which are made from fabric.

▲ In the space below, draw a picture of your bedroom. Put in all the things which are made from fabric.

▲ Talk about your picture with your friends.

▲ ESSENTIALS FOR SCIENCE: Paper and fabrics

▲ Name _____

What are you wearing today?

You will need: a hand lens; a pencil.

▲ In the frame below, draw a picture of yourself wearing the clothes you have on today.

▲ Find out what your clothes are made from.

▲ Label your drawing with the names of the clothes and what they are made from.

▲ Find out which are made from natural fibres, manufactured fibres or a mixture of both. You may need help with this.

▲ ESSENTIALS FOR SCIENCE: Paper and fabrics

▲ Name _____

Fabric, thread and fibre ⚠

You will need: a piece of sacking, hessian or other coarse woven fabric; a hand lens; a microscope; scissors; glue.

▲ Take a square of fabric about 10cm x 10cm. Use a hand lens to see how it is woven together.

▲ Pull out a piece of thread and look at it with a hand lens to see how it is made.

▲ Untwist the thread and look at one fibre under a microscope.

▲ Stick a piece of fabric, thread and fibre in the spaces below. Write down words to describe them.

Fabric _____

Thread _____

Fibre _____

▲ Look at a different kind of fabric in the same way. What are the differences between the two fabrics? How are they the same?

▲ ESSENTIALS FOR SCIENCE: Paper and fabrics

▲ Name _____

Types of fabrics ⚠

You will need: a hand lens; examples of knitted, woven and tangled fabrics; scissors; glue.

Fabrics are made from fibres which are interlaced together. They can be:

| Knitted | Woven | Tangled |

▲ Use a hand lens and the pictures shown above to help you find one fabric of each kind.

▲ What can you find out about the different kinds of fabric?
- Try stretching them.
- Hold them up to the light. What can you see?
- Unravel some of the fabric to see how the fibres are interlaced.

▲ Share what you have discovered with your friends.

▲ Stick examples below and label them.

_____   _____   _____

▲ ESSENTIALS FOR SCIENCE: Paper and fabrics   23

▲ Name _____

How strong are threads? ⚠

You will need: 30cm lengths of thread made from cotton, wool and nylon or other kinds of manufactured threads; a hook fixed in a low position to a wall; a small bucket; marbles or weights; sticky tape; a pencil.

▲Sort out the threads into sets of wool threads, cotton threads and manufactured threads.

▲Compare the look and feel of the threads.

▲Test the strength of the threads by tying one end to the hook and the other to the handle of the bucket. Gradually put weights in the bucket until the thread breaks.

▲Stick a sample of thread on to paper and write down how much the thread held.

▲Test the other threads. Did they all break in the same way?
  • Were you unable to break some?
  • Which set had the strongest threads?
  • Are the threads as strong when wet?

▲ Name _____

Weaving

You will need: threads (knitting and carpet yarns); cardboard about 20cm x 25cm; scissors; craft needle; sticky tape.

▲Cut notches in the top and bottom of the cardboard.

▲Wind thread through the notches, pull it tightly and stick down the ends with sticky tape.

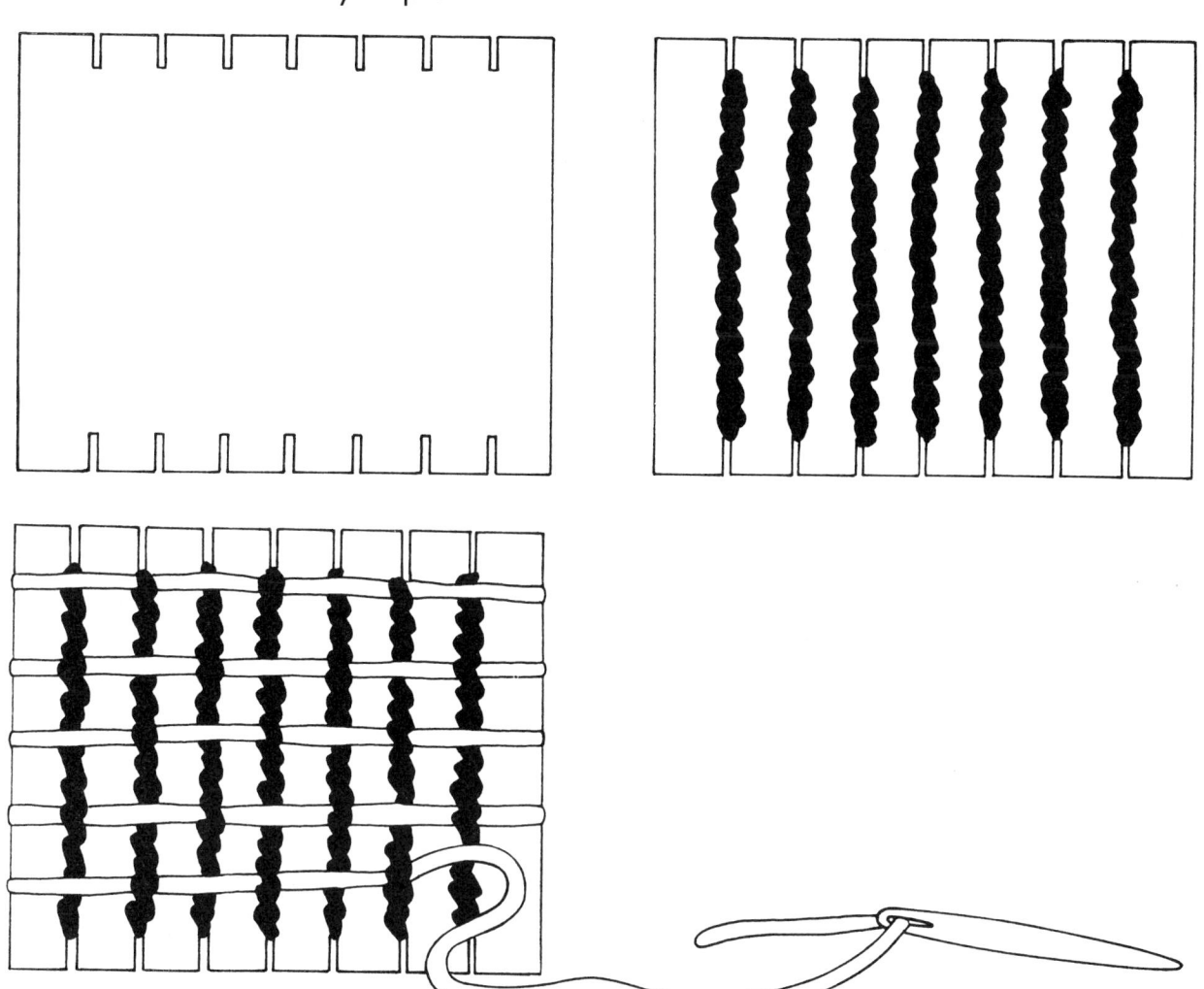

▲Choose different kinds of threads and weave them in and out of the threads on the cardboard.

▲When you have finished, cut the thread on the cardboard at the back of the card and pull the card away.

▲Knot the ends so that the weaving will not come undone.

▲Look at your piece of fabric. How does the weaving change with the use of different threads?

▲ Name _____

Keeping warm and keeping cool

▲ Look at the drawings of clothes below.

▲ Put a red ring round the clothes which keep you warm and a blue ring round the clothes which help you to keep cool.

- T-shirt
- coat
- shorts
- woolly hat
- socks
- gloves
- sun hat
- bikini
- scarf

▲ Make a list of the clothes you are wearing today.

▲ Are they clothes that keep you warm or cool? What is the weather like today?

▲ ESSENTIALS FOR SCIENCE: Paper and fabrics

▲ Name _____

Which fabric keeps you warm? ⚠

You will need: three pieces of fabric the same size, such as wool, cotton and nylon; four drinks cans; a funnel; water which is hot but **not** boiling.

▲ Wrap one can in each type of fabric.

▲ Ask an adult to pour the same amount of hot water into each can. Leave them for 15 minutes.

▲ Take the covers off the cans. Which can feels the warmest?

▲ Draw the coverings on the pictures below and write down what happened.

▲ Which fabric would keep you warm in winter?

ESSENTIALS FOR SCIENCE: Paper and fabrics

▲ Name _____

Wet fabric and dry fabric ⚠

You will need: two pieces of fabric which are exactly the same; cold water; hot, but **not** boiling, water; a table fork; a hand lens.

▲Use your senses to make observations about your fabric.
- What does it look and feel like?
- What does it smell like?

▲Keep one piece of fabric dry. Wet the other with cold water. What changes do you notice?

▲Put the wet fabric in hot water. After a few minutes take it out with a fork. Are there any more changes?

▲Write down what you have found out.

Dry fabric Wet fabric

▲When your fabric dries, find out if it is the same as it was before.

▲Do all fabrics behave in the same way?

▲ ESSENTIALS FOR SCIENCE: Paper and fabrics

▲ Name _____

Drying fabric

You will need: four pieces of fabric which are exactly the same; clothes pegs; washing line; a timer.

▲ Find out which is the best place to dry fabric. Think of different kinds of places. You could choose inside, outside in the shade or outside in the sun and wind.

▲ Hang each wet piece of fabric in the same way. Put on the timer. Time how long each piece took to dry.

▲ Fill in the chart to show what happens.

Inside	Outside in the sun
Outside in shade	Outside in sun and wind

▲ Look at the chart. Where would clothes dry most quickly?

▲ Compare what happened with other fabrics. Which fabric dried the quickest?

▲ ESSENTIALS FOR SCIENCE: Paper and fabrics

▲ Name _____

Which fabric for a waterproof hat?

You will need: 10cm squares of fabric such as wool, cotton, nylon, denim, net, PVC, waxed linen; a teaspoon; coloured water; a hand lens.

▲ Choose a piece of fabric. What does it look and feel like? Do you think it will make a waterproof hat?

▲ Place the fabric on white paper and pour on a spoonful of coloured water.

▲ Record what happens in the chart below.

▲ Test the other fabrics in the same way.

Type of fabric	Water soaks through	Water spreads out	Water stays on surface	Will it make a water-proof hat?

▲ Which fabric will make a waterproof hat?

▲ Draw and label a picture of yourself in waterproof clothes. What are the clothes made from?

▲ ESSENTIALS FOR SCIENCE: Paper and fabrics

▲ Name _____

Which fabrics are hard wearing? ⚠

You will need: pieces of fabric such as cotton, wool, nylon, denim, net, PVC; drawing pins; a board; a sandpaper block (wood wrapped in sandpaper); glue.

▲ Examine the fabrics. Which do you think will be hard wearing?

▲ Pin one fabric to the board.

▲ Rub the fabric with the sandpaper block 20 times. Rub it in the same direction each time. What happens to the fabric?

▲ Test the other fabrics in the same way.

▲ Record the results below.

Example of the fabric	Number of rubs	Fabric after the test	Any other test

▲ Can you think of any other way to test for hard wearing?

▲ Which is the most hard wearing? Can you think why?

▲ ESSENTIALS FOR SCIENCE: Paper and fabrics

▲ Name _____

Litter: paper and fabrics ⚠️

You will need: two collections of paper and fabric litter which are exactly the same.

▲ Go round the school grounds to find out if there are any signs of paper or fabric litter. Do not handle the litter. What do you notice?

▲ Make two collections of paper and fabrics. Put one in a box inside and put the other outdoors, perhaps under a hedge.

▲ Leave the litter for two weeks.

▲ After two weeks compare the two sets. Wear polythene gloves to handle the litter.

▲ What changes do you notice? What has caused the changes?

▲ ESSENTIALS FOR SCIENCE: Paper and fabrics